Intelligence:

Discover the 65 Traits of Intelligence

Dr. Alexander G. Alemis

ISBN 9781671569300

Dr. Alexander G. Alemis

Dr. Alexander G. Alemis is a dentist in Chicago, Illinois. He has been practicing dentistry since 1986 and is the founder of the Family Dental Care Group, a multi-group practice. He is an accomplished businessman and author.

[illegible]

[illegible]

ACKNOWLEDGMENTS

I would like to acknowledge many people who have helped me throughout my life. My parents, schoolteachers, colleagues, staff, and many friends.

I would especially like to thank my family and my staff for putting up with my crazy schedule.

DISCLAIMER

This book contains the thoughts and ideas of the author. Some of the concepts presented here are abstract and subjective and represent the opinions and experiences of the author. It is not intended to be a dogmatic[1] presentation nor is it a scientific thesis[2]. It is not intended to counsel anyone with specific issues or needs. It is up to the reader to agree or disagree with the materials presented.

---

[1]Dogmatic: to claim it's the only way and no other way
[2] Thesis: a statement or position put forth to be proven

My Philosophy:

Help yourself by helping others.

Nobody does it alone. Accept help,

help others and pass it on.

If you want to be educated, then educate others.

If you want to retain knowledge and

expand it, then make

others knowledgeable about what is important.

If you want to walk free, then free others.

MY VISION FOR THIS BOOK

My vision for you in regard to this book is threefold:

a. **To feel like you got a bargain**. Whatever money you paid to obtain this book I want you to feel that you got a bargain even if you paid thousands, since the knowledge gained will be with you for the rest of your life. This is a timeless book that you can pass on to your children and grandchildren.

b. **To read the book many times** as the information contained here is condensed and a lot of it is totally new. Read it several times over the course of the next months or years and increase your overall intelligence.

c. While studying the book **look up any words in the dictionary** that you don't fully understand. Don't assume you know them if they are not perfectly clear for you.

I thank you for buying my book. Have fun reading it!

INTRODUCTION

The subject of intelligence has been covered in many books and by many authors throughout the ages. The measuring of intelligence has been attempted by many educators, psychologists, and employers.

When we speak of intelligence we think of ability, logic, smarts, swift handlings, ethics, survival, beauty, and a myriad of other things.

But how do we really define intelligence? Is it book smarts? Is it leadership ability? Is it the ability to make money? What exactly is this thing called intelligence?

The best definition of intelligence for me is the following:

INTELLIGENCE IS THE ABILITY TO SOLVE LIFE'S PROBLEMS AND CAPITALIZE ON OPPORTUNITIES PRESENTED IN LIFE AND THEREFORE OBTAIN OPTIMAL SURVIVAL.

Said otherwise, what good is this thing called intelligence if it can't help you solve life's problems and capitalize on the opportunities available and therefore have a good life?

If we accept the above definition for intelligence **we must then accept that intelligence must be more than just one thing, as it takes**

many different abilities to solve life's problems and to be able to recognize and take advantage of the opportunities presented.

As I will show in this book, intelligence is indeed composed of several parts, which people possess unequally. Some of us possess only a few, others many; but very few possess most of the intelligence traits portrayed in this book. To make this point let's look at a few intelligence giants in our history.

Albert Einstein and Nikola Tesla, most people would agree, were considered two of the greatest minds who ever walked on the planet. Yet, the first one's family life leaves a lot to be desired, and he is forever connected with the development of the atom bomb, which gave men the ability to destroy the planet. Tesla on the other hand was used by far less able minds and died alone in a hotel with his inventions and patents up for grabs by his enemies. Pythagoras, another great giant of intelligence, was very arrogant and was killed during a riot in Crotona.

Although these people possessed many of the intelligence traits they did not possess all of them, as you will discover by reading this book.

How was it determined that these abilities or characteristics are intelligence traits? It was based on the original definition of intelligence, which is the ability to solve life's problems and capitalize on life's opportunities.

Using that as a guide I was able to break intelligence down to **65 traits or parts** that I list and explain in the following pages. Why 65? Well, that's how many I discovered as I was researching the subject.

It all started a few years ago, when I wrote a small essay on intelligence for my office executive course, explaining that intelligence was more than just one or two things. When I originally wrote the article, I had come up with twelve intelligence characteristics. Subsequently, I got very interested in the subject and wrote more about it. As I kept researching and writing over the next thirteen months my essay turned out to be a book, as I discovered that intelligence is composed of many more traits, 65 in total, which I share with you here.

As you read the book, find out how many of these traits you possess, to what degree and which you need to improve upon. Some of these intelligence traits are innate, yet others can be acquired by learning about them. Every one of these can be improved upon if one works diligently on improving them. **Your intelligence should greatly improve just by reading this book**.

THE 65 TRAITS OF INTELLIGENCE

Chapter A

School or Book Smarts Intelligence

1. Duplication or Book Intelligence

This is the ability to duplicate information such as schoolwork. In this capacity people vary greatly. Some duplicate materials with what seems like a photographic memory, while others have to read the materials ten times in order to remember just a part of it. Further, some people seem to be able to memorize the materials better if they hear it, others if they see it, and most can memorize it better if they actually apply it.

How fast can you duplicate something? It certainly depends on this type of ability, but **if you understand the meaning of all the words and symbols you are reading fully**, it will make all the difference. How about speed reading? If you don't know the full meaning of the words and symbols in the subject you are reading, forget about it. You will speed read without understanding.

«Αρχη παιδευσεως η των ονοματων επισκεψις»

"The beginning of education is the exact study of the meaning of the words."
-Antesthenis
(Ancient Greek Philosopher)

In addition, if you have a great foundation on a subject you will be able to read the materials faster, fully duplicate its meaning and be able to memorize it better as well.

One of the mistakes we make at school is to study for exams and not for the purpose of fully understanding and learning the material, i.e., establish the foundation. The entire school system is set up like that.

I do not possess the ability to remember things without understanding or for no good reason to do so, but others do. My wife can remember the phone numbers we had when we first got married 25 years ago; my mind, on the other hand, discards and forgets numbers as soon as I feel I don't have to remember them.

Any subject has basic concepts in it, which I call pillars or foundations, and if you learn these, everything else goes fast after that. A good example of this for me was organic chemistry. During the second semester, although some of my classmates were having a hard time, I was getting an easy A, because I had worked really hard and truly understood the basic concepts of organic chemistry as given during the first semester.

«Γλωσσα πρωτη μαθησεων, δι ης
εξεστι τας αλλας μαθειν»

"The study of language is the first study (the foundation), which enables you to learn everything else."

-Antisthenes

2. Calculative or Mathematical Intelligence

This trait pertains to the ability to calculate things in one's mind and come up with proper answers, especially in regard to solving math problems.

In grammar school my teacher would ask math questions of the entire class, and it was a game of who was to get the answer first. One of my classmates could calculate all sorts of equations in his head very quickly. His calculative or mathematical intelligence was very impressive and certainly higher than that of the rest of us, several of whom are now scientists. He was exceptional at this type of intelligence, but not very good at others, as he ended up not being very successful in life.

Some people have this ability in spades and they can do all sorts of tricks, which makes them look superhuman, at least in this area. It has been written that Einstein could visualize math equations in his head and was able to solve them mentally.

This trait also involves the ability to judge math or equation problems as seen in life or even on a computer. For example, some people punch numbers in a computer to figure out say 15% of $1,000 and immediately know it is wrong when they get an answer of $1,150, whereas others take it as correct because it came from the computer.

3. Willingness to Seek Out Secondhand Knowledge Intelligence

Secondhand knowledge means knowledge or information you get besides direct observation. It is the documented observations and literature research of other people. These come in the form of books, films, discussions, meetings, seminars, etc.

Some people have access to great secondhand knowledge sources, but others who live in rural areas of third world countries have none. Of the ones who have secondhand knowledge in abundance some do not bother to avail themselves to it; others take full advantage of it.

We all have heard the phrase: **Readers are leaders**. That is because even if you possess a brilliant mind you will never be able to know everything just by your direct observation. You need to read books and get information from other sources to have a great education about subjects in life. Besides historical facts, the reading of good books will give you invaluable knowledge about human nature across the globe that covers eons of human history. This will help raise your overall intelligence in your field and about life in general.

Regarding secondhand knowledge though, it is important to understand that there is a lot of useless or damaging information out there. In fact, a lot of books can at best be a waste of time. It is therefore critical to get the right books, not just any books. **The ability to pick the important from the unimportant data is an intelligence trait in itself.** This would fall under the Judgment and Discriminatory Intelligences as you will see in the following pages.

Chapter B

Somatic Intelligence

4. Somatic[3] Intelligence

This is body ability. Some people can maneuver their bodies in a way that makes them look superhuman, yet others can barely catch a ball.

To be able to handle a ball in a professional game, such as basketball, and earn millions, or handle a weapon in war adroitly and win a fight, is part of this intelligence. Certain people have very capable minds, yet they can't coordinate their bodies to do much.

In the not too distant past, lack of somatic intelligence meant death as the body did most of the work, unlike today where machines are facilitating our everyday living.

Even today though, athletes (especially professional ball players) and artists continue to get rewarded handsomely for their somatic abilities. **This part of intelligence can also be called the mind and body coordination.**

It is very interesting how some people can have great somatic abilities in one area, yet not in another. Somatic ability/intelligence can be greatly improved with sports. Children should be exposed to all types of sports and try out as many as they can so that they can discover where their somatic talent lies. Great somatic ability boosts one's confidence in life.

---

[3] Soma = body (Greek)

5. Health Conscious Intelligence

The ancient Greeks had a phrase: **"healthy mind in a healthy body."** Otherwise said, your mind will be healthy if it resides in a healthy body and vice versa.

I had classmates at school whom I thought of as very intelligent because they were book smart, who did drugs or got drunk often. Drugs alter your personality and destroy your judgment. They can wipe out any other ability you might have, despite arguments by some groups to the contrary. I noticed a change of behavior in my kids after they were on antibiotics for just a week; I can imagine what it would be like if they were on mind-altering drugs.

Doing drugs or destroying your body by other means such as smoking, lack of exercise, or eating bad foods is not intelligent and will not help you survive well in life.

Life is a very competitive game; we need all the advantages we can possibly get. Why anyone would want to fry their neurons and dull their perceptions is beyond me.

Even if you amass great wealth it does you no good if you are sick because you didn't take care of your body. Severely damaged lungs due to smoking are not fixable no matter the amount of money you possess.

My wife would also add that staying up and writing books instead of sleeping can be unintelligent even for the most intelligent authors.

Chapter C

Emotional Intelligence

6. Emotional Intelligence

Can you handle the emotional ups and downs life gives you or do you fall apart at the first difficulty? In short, can you handle your emotions?

Logic must precede your emotions; otherwise you will lead an unhappy life.

If you find yourself sexually attracted to someone but he/she is married with kids and seems to be happy in the marriage, can you handle your emotions or do you create a mess of your life and others around you?

Some people can handle all sorts of emotional upsets and continue to push forward with a smile on their faces; others go crazy when something goes wrong or when someone looks at them cross-eyed and even commit murder, which lands them in jail.

It has been written that Christ preached that when one is slapping you, you are not to fight back but you should turn the other cheek. At first glance this appears to be anti-survival, as it seems to say, let the other guy beat you up. How does this teaching make any sense? How could this type of behavior have any workability?

What I believe Christ was teaching here is the concept that force begets force and when you put force against another force, the two forces collide and both people get hurt. What Christ suggested instead was to apply emotional intelligence and let the opponent's force go through don't hit against it or resist it so that no crushing can take place.

The idea is not to get beaten up, but rather to avoid the head-on conflict, be it either verbal or physical and avoid the collision. Instead let the force go through and find no resistance to create anything of consequence. For example, if one is yelling at you and he is looking for a fight you have two choices: to fight him or not to fight him. If you fight him, even if you win, you will have some losses by ripple consequences. His friends may come after you later or you might suffer a few bruises yourself. If you decide to let his anger find no resistance, and claim to understand his viewpoint, his upset will find no reciprocation and therefore no fuel to enlarge it and it will die down sooner or later.

In another example, which is a little abstract, let's imagine the effect of a bullet shot by an opponent. If you put something in front of it to resist it, the bullet will cause trouble, it will have an effect. If you let the bullet go into space, it will be of no consequence.

Turn the other cheek is a figure of speech meaning to be emotionally intelligent and don't put force against force.

This is the type of intelligence I believe Christ was referring to when He said to turn the other cheek. He did not mean for you to give up, but rather not to engage in petty fights, or silly spats but rather, to just let it go and work toward your meaningful, long-term goals. Handle the other person or persons with reason and understanding and not by putting up force . . . unless of course there is no other option. However, you should be intelligent enough to have created other options.

7. Playfulness Intelligence

Can you be a childlike dreamer? Can you be light and have fun? Can you relax and let your hair down? Playfulness is an important ability to possess. After all, life is a game; to have fun playing it, is what it is ultimately all about. It says so in our Declaration of Independence... "the pursuit of happiness."

Look at some very successful people's behavior toward life, current and past. Look at Bill Gates, Warren Buffet, Lionel Messi, Michael Jordan, or Pelé; they are and were very playful creating on the canvas of life and having fun doing so.

I have met some very successful people, most of whom are very wealthy. They are like kids having fun in creating things in life no matter their age.

What do all these people have in common? They are able. They possess most of the intelligence traits, which makes them very able. Said otherwise, the abler you are the more real fun you can have in life. **So, go ahead, increase your overall intelligence and have more fun.**

All the intelligence traits mentioned in this book dovetail together and this one dovetails especially well with the ability to handle people. It is easier to handle people if you exude lightheartedness about yourself and life in general. Due to your playfulness and easygoing spirit people will like you, trust you, and perform better for you.

8. Think for Yourself Intelligence

In life, in order to stand on your own two feet, you must be able to think for yourself and act based on your own judgment and not be run by other people's ideas via rumors or bad data. In order to do that you must be comfortable with yourself and your own critical thinking ability.

The majority of people cannot stand being alone or to have to think for themselves. They need company, music, the TV, something or somebody at all times. They are directed and led by a collective emotional thought process instead of their own compass. They follow this collective thought process to wherever it leads them. **They would rather be wrong than alone**[4]. They do not feel unique among others but a part of a big wheel that is turning beyond their control. They have decided that they possess no original thoughts or ideas rather they repeat what they hear or see on the media, the books they read, or whatever their friends are discussing.

---

[4]Rather be wrong than alone: They would rather not speak out about an injustice or something that is done wrong than risk being alienated by their own peers.

If these people stopped and thought for a second, they would realize that they do have the ability to think for themselves and that not all things presented by authorities are accurate. Unfortunately, most people don't even think that they should question anything presented by authorities.

Perhaps lack of this intelligence trait alone is the biggest problem in our world today. This is the reason we get what we call mob mentality.

The world's great geniuses throughout history possessed the ability to think for themselves and they saw futures and realities others never dreamed of. **They could constantly hear the beat of their own drummer and nothing could distract them from that. I advise you do the same.**

9. Patience Intelligence

How could patience be an intelligence trait when in fact, most giants of intelligence were and are impatient? Highly intelligent people want to get things done now, but in order to be able to solve life's problems **you need to realize that everyone and everything in life has its own speed.** Realizing that and waiting patiently during the maturation stage is a great intelligence trait. You can speed things up, but only by following their own course and tuning in to their speed and thought process.

The best example are children. We try to put all children in the same learning speed (school years), which is so unfair to them. Where children come from is a religious question. The nonreligious answer given in our society is: "from their mother's womb of course, and they are all starting fresh from the same point." But alas, just look at them. They are all so different. Some it seems know so much the minute they are born; others act like they know nothing. Therefore, they should not all be put through the same schooling speed, but should follow their own maturation process. Some children can finish grammar school in four years, others may need eight. The same holds true for the rest of their schooling.

Everything in life has its own speed and process. Humans need nine months, give or take a few weeks, to mature in the womb. It is just the way it is. Most things, unlike fetus growth, you can speed up, but only if you tune in on their wavelength and engage them at their speed first and lead them from there; otherwise, they will reject you as not being real to them or will simply not understand you, which has the same outcome. This is a weak area for me as I feel people should understand what I understand and should see what I see. Since they do not, I tend to be critical of people.

Lack of patience and understanding with people is the fastest way to lose friends and gain many adversaries. Everyone and everything in life is at a certain level and you need to address them from there. Otherwise you will not be real to them and they will consider you an adversary. That level could be one hundred steps lower than what you think it should be. Well, you have to start from there, not skip any steps and exhibit great patience.

You have heard the phrase "patience is a virtue." Yes, it is. It is an intelligence trait.

Chapter D

Discipline and Goal Intelligence

10. Goal and Perseverance Intelligence

Life is only livable by having goals. Therefore, having goals is a form of intelligence. Once a person stops having goals he either gets in trouble or dies. It is true every time. If you plan on retiring, then make sure you set up new goals, otherwise you will be unhappy, regardless of circumstances.

Perseverance toward a goal is the ability to just keep pushing toward it regardless of difficulties. It is the ability to keep the goal in sight regardless of what is happening around you.

In life, there are short-term goals and long-term goals. Becoming a doctor requires over 20 years of schooling. That's a lot of time considering that these are the best body years in someone's life. Do you stay the course for such a long-term goal or do you abandon it when you realize how long it takes?

In another example, some of us write books in an attempt to straighten out the wrongs of the world, but such work is usually not popular and it can take generations for any effort to culminate into something useful and to create a fundamental change. So, do you bother pushing toward that direction or just forget about it thinking:

"What's the use? People will never change; I'll just worry about me for now"?

The ability to stay the course and persevere toward a worthy goal or goals is dependent on this type of intelligence.

11. Discipline or Will Power Intelligence

This is similar to perseverance and emotional intelligence but it is a distinctly different trait. I will present this by the use of several examples that contain the use of this type of intelligence.

Example 1: Let's say you had a good meal and feel good about it, but now the waiter brings you the tray of desserts. The chocolate mousse looks incredible and one of your friends says that you must try it, no matter what. You know very well that any additional calories will kill your diet. Do you order the dessert or pass on it?

Example 2: Tomorrow you have an important appointment, but the movie you are watching on television is mesmerizing. Do you turn the TV off and go to bed in time to get a good night's sleep or do you stay up until 2 a.m. watching the movie?

Example 3: You are in the middle of an important meeting or you are performing a task in your profession but something has rattled you or your body feels tired or achy. Do you act rattled, tired, or awkward or do you maintain a professional demeanor and complete the task at hand successfully and with a smile on your face?

How you behave on all of the above scenarios has to do with your discipline or will power intelligence.

Discipline is one of those parts of intelligence that is directly influenced by your education or training and most of all by your peers. If you want to be disciplined, then be around other disciplined people.

12. Commitment and Long-Term Mentality Intelligence

The television portrays personalities who, despite the fact that they jump around a lot during their lifetime, still find great success. It shows them going through multiple divorces, changing numerous jobs, careers, etc. They make millions, lose millions, and then remake them all over again. That might make good television, but I know no one who is successful with this type of behavior. Undoubtedly some can pull it off, but the overwhelming majority of people who lack commitment in life end up losing traction and never get very far.

All people whom I know to be successful have made long-term commitments in their lives and have stuck with them. They are married to the same spouse, they are in the same career, they have their business in the same location, etc.

Success in life requires commitment and perseverance; commitment to a family, a career or to a particular location and space. You need to be there for a long time in order to gain trust with your customers and colleagues and in order to be successful.

When you do that, success becomes geometric and not arithmetic, meaning it does not add 1+1+1 but multiplies such as 2 x 4 x 8, etc.

Otherwise said, at age 60 you might earn 10 times more than what you earned at age 30 even adjusting for inflation.

This is true in business as well as in family life. If you get divorced two times just for the mere fact that you had to split your energy and wealth twice, it will almost guarantee that you never reach any level of financial success and your kids will just drift off.

If the above is true, it is imperative to think through your decisions before you commit to a spouse, a career, or a business venture. If you make a mistake, then make the change early in life, otherwise you will have a difficult task toward any level of success.

Intelligent people know the above and don't jump to different careers on a whim pretending to be important and assuming that it will all work out. They set long-term goals and stick with them. It is what many intelligent families have done over several generations . . . families who have kept the wealth and know-how about a service or a product over hundreds of years and are running very successful ventures. Some of which are even multibillion dollar businesses. Examples? Many. Have you heard of Breitling Watches, Trader Joes, or the Wallenbergs in Sweden? They are all private multibillion dollar family businesses.

Commitment intelligence means to have a good thorough plan and stick to it; and remember, **boring work that leads to success is very exciting!**

13. Survivability Intelligence

A strong desire and willingness to survive despite all odds is an ability, possessed by few, despite appearances.

The majority of people given a good rope can be coaxed along to suicide. I know many will disagree with this, but look around and see all the non-survival things people do despite claims by them to the contrary. In the face of adversity, people give up and get out of the fight very easily. They divorce, do drugs, quit their job, drop out of school, etc.

Rocky Balboa, in the movie "Rocky" did not give up, but eventually won because he possessed this type of intelligence. This can also be called the belief that you are unkillable and that you will get up again and again no matter what is done to you. A showing of unkillability or an unwillingness to die puts the enemy in apathy.

I don't like pain so I would not want to be Rocky Balboa, but you have to hand it to him. His perseverance to just stand there and take it made him unkillable, which put his opponent in apathy; Rocky persevered and won the boxing match.

In many ways, life is like Rocky's opponent, it keeps on pounding on us constantly despite what the *feel-good movies* show or the *good story books* tells us. One wrong move and your life can be upside down. A driving accident, a bad marriage, a temper day at work, one overlooked account, a walk in the wrong neighborhood, a slip on the ice, etc., is all it takes and you are in for it.

It takes a very strong desire to survive and a strong willingness to make things go right. Also faith in yourself that you will make things go right, regardless of what life throws at you. Regarding this concept, people who had to make it on their own, the ones who pulled themselves up by their own bootstraps, so to speak, have a big advantage over others who had things handed to them.

This trait is similar to the Goal or Perseverance Intelligence, but different in the sense that it has the deeper meaning of survivability in it with or without goals. It includes the belief that one survives the death of the body and continues to live on as himself despite others trying to convince him otherwise. This belief alone gives one a higher degree of hope, purpose, and ethics.

Chapter E

Social or People Intelligence

14. Proper Handling of People Intelligence

This is the ability to connect with and handle people. Some people seem to have the gift of making friends and fruitful connections wherever they go, while others can't get a friend if their lives depended on it.

In a disagreement, can you see the other guy's viewpoint? Can you allow him/her to save face and be diplomatic about your handling of the situation?

The word diplomat is derived from the two Greek words Dio and Mati: dio = two, mati = eye. It literally means to have double eyes. In other words, to be a diplomat means to have the ability to see things from the other person's eyes as well as your own.

Can you be a true diplomat? That's a high-level intelligence. It does not mean to just be politically correct, but rather to be able to handle people in a way where they feel understood and willing to trust you. Can you do that? This ability is critical for a CEO of a company or the leader of an organization or a country.

People are not machines easily understood using math or social engineering. We are all different with our own unique characteristics and opinions. Handling people well means doing the right thing; or the thing that works for the people involved at each given time and circumstance.

Pythagoras, possibly the greatest mathematician of all time, was despised by a lot of people due to his arrogant demeanor. He had some very arrogant viewpoints such as that he would not allow his students to engage in any discussions or have any opinions during the first five years of their studies. These were students who paid him handsomely to attend his school. He was killed during a riot.

Nothing is more important to your long term success than your ability to handle people.

Following are three different types of philosophical approaches (executive policies) I use to train my executives on handling people. I think you will find them useful.

a. Approach People from Their Good Side

It is said that when dealing with people you can approach them with honey or vinegar. I took this concept a little further and created the following diagram of a person's mind. The mind can be considered to have two parts. One side has good things in it and the other side has bad things in it. Here is my graphic depiction of it.

A Person's Mind

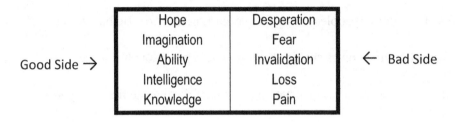

	Hope	Desperation	
	Imagination	Fear	
Good Side →	Ability	Invalidation	← Bad Side
	Intelligence	Loss	
	Knowledge	Pain	

Study the diagram for a minute and realize that people's minds can be categorized as such. We all have good and happy thoughts about ourselves and others as well as bad and destructive ones.

When you are engaging people, you have two choices. You can engage them from one side of their mind or the other. If you engage them a little bit from both sides, you get a mixed result.

What you get from people depends on which side you engage them from. If you are nice to someone, you are engaging him from the good side of his mind and you get the best of him. As an example, when you walk into your office in the morning and you compliment your executive Jill on the great job she did yesterday at her presentation and tell her how you intend to have her do more of them since she proved to be good at it, she will most likely feel great about your acknowledgment and give you even better presentations.

On the other hand, if you are mean and invalidate people you are engaging them from the bad side of their mind and as a consequence, you will get the worst of them.

The majority of the people, once engaged from their good side, will be nicer to you and will give you their best possible effort.

A minority will be rather neutral but will not be mean to you.

About 5% of the people will continue to be unkind to you no matter how nice you are to them, although they might be covert about it. Let this 5% be other people's friends or employees.

b. Take Full Responsibility for the Relationship

When dealing with other people socially or in a working relationship we can categorize all the possible interchanges we can have with them into three different basic approaches shown below.

i. You take 100% responsibility for the other person

In this approach you go out of your way to get him to want to work with you and help him succeed, in spite of himself. Example: A coworker does not say "Good Morning" back to you after you said "Good Morning" to him. You find out why and handle it. Regardless, you keep saying "Good Morning" to him because that's the right thing to do and assume the viewpoint that it will all work out and you will have a harmonious relationship at the end. In this approach each person involved takes 100% responsibility for the other regardless of circumstances. I know this is a tall order, but it is the sanest approach.

ii. 50/50

You take 50% responsibility for the relationship. Your modus operandi is: "I am doing my share. You do your share and I will meet you halfway." Example: You say "Good Morning" once, and if the other person does not respond back to you, you ignore him until he/she responds. Don't try to find out why he did not say "Good Morning" back, that's not your responsibility. Let him figure it out, you did your part, you went halfway as necessary. Let him meet you at the halfway point as he should, such as saying good morning back to you before you say anything more to him. This is the most popular approach in our society.

iii. Kiss my @*)

This approach is along the lines of: "I am sitting back and you come to me" type of thing. "You prove yourself to me," "You show me why I should help you," "I am the boss and I don't have to be nice to anyone. I give you a job, that's good enough", or "You cater to me and if you don't like it, get out."

Approaches two and three above have limited workability and do not present for harmonious relationships.

Do option *i*, keep doing it and expect the other guy to behave the same way sooner or later. The majority of people will respond to you the same way within a short time. The rest will show themselves as antisocial and you will then know who they are and you decide how you want to handle them. But you will not know who they are for sure unless you keep using approach ***i*** in handling all the people around you regardless of their behavior.

c. Despite shortcomings, find and use people's talents for mutual benefit

Sometimes the planet feels like an asylum and at other times it is like the patients are running it. Friends, family members, teachers, and in general people you think should know better do crazy things. Our political leaders, who are supposed to be the best leaders we can find, have put our country in enormous debt pretending it is all normal.

As you can see then, we can find faults with almost anyone, and point them out all day long, just like the media do. But there is no benefit in that unless you are in the business of selling chaos like the media do.

Although it is true that all people have flaws and some more than others, I find that most people I meet, despite their flaws, have some kind of talent or a *know-how* I can use to our mutual benefit.

Here is how I suggest you apply this concept:

1. Know that all people have issues. No one is perfect.
2. See the issues in each person for what they are; don't sugarcoat them.
3. Look and find a talent or know-how in each person.
4. Then ask yourself: "Can this person's faults be detrimental to me?"
    a. If so, let this person be someone else's *"friend."*
    b. If not, then engage **this person's talent or talents and know-hows and use them toward a win-win situation.** This is emphasized in bold print because most of the time people will not be able to offer their talents and bring about a mutually beneficial condition; you need to do that for them.

The moral of this crazy world is this: without ignoring people's faults and while protecting yourself from them, find people's talents and know-hows and use them for mutual benefit.

The above policies are condensed simplifications from my observations and studies of different subjects in life. They are not *the works of the mind* but they have served me well in my dealings with people and especially in training my executives. Try them out and see how they work for you.

15. Communication Intelligence

«Δίανοια καί λὸγος ταύτὸν»
("One's speech shows his intelligence level")

--Plato

To be able to communicate your thoughts and ideas to other people whereby they can fully understand you and be persuaded to some degree to do something because of it, is a great ability needed by all and especially the leaders of our world. **This,** by the way, **seems to be the most rewarded ability in our society. The best paid people in the world today are people who have great communication skills.**

Successful CEOs'[4], actors, politicians, musicians and artists all have excellent communication skills. It would be impossible to get elevated to a high-profile position in any field without this ability.

Why do we reward these people highly? **Because they communicate to us in such a way where we feel that they understand us and that we understand them.**

Our appreciation for good communication is such that people who have great communication skills, but no talents can fool us with

[4] CEO – Chief Executive Officer – The top position in a company.

their rhetoric. Because of that a lot of times we follow or elect leaders who are able to persuade us that they can do the job and as a consequence we overlook the ones who have actually exhibited the ability to do it, if the latter ones are not good communicators. It is a shame **when an able person can't communicate well**. He might be great for the job, but if we can't understand him we will not take his advice, and certainly we will not want to be part of his group or buy from him and therefore not reward him . . . **to the detriment of all.**

Today in America and everywhere else in the world for that matter, the entire "west" has been conquered and all "the land" belongs to someone. Therefore, anything you want in life you have to get from someone else, or otherwise said, everything you want in life you need to persuade others to give it to you via exchange and that depends greatly on your ability to communicate well with them. You must be able to communicate in such a way whereby the other person or group feels like they understand you and want to follow your advice and or buy your service or product.

Great communicators are giants among humans.

16. Humility Intelligence

Humility: The ability to fully appreciate the importance of something and or life in general as it relates to you and the other parts and elements of the environment (my definition).

In short, humility means **correct appraisal;** as in appraising life and people correctly. To appraise something correctly means to fully assess it for what it truly is without adding or subtracting from it and to further appraise yourself in relationship to it and other things and people around you.

Arrogance is the opposite of humility. It is the dismissing of the importance of something or someone. Arrogance cuts one's ability to learn and the chance to connect with people. Arrogant people make mistakes and fail due to their incorrect appraisal of situations or people.

A know-it-all will never learn another thing. A know-best will never see another person's point of view.

The #1 reason intelligent people end up not being successful or fall from grace is arrogance.

Humility does not mean: I am a lowly servant. That definition is for the birds and dangerous to your survival. Humility is the understanding of the fact that life is just so vast and complex whereby tremendous abilities are needed to even navigate through it, let alone succeed. I tell my staff that in life nothing is simple, engage everything with respect and even reverence. Just walking up or down a flight of stairs involves phenomenal biomechanical systems and a great deal of coordination and abilities of the body and mind during the entire process.

Life is not to be feared, but one must appreciate the fact that it's so much larger than any one of us.

17. Appreciation Intelligence

There is a phrase in a song that says "Do you like what life is showing you?" Yes, this a type of intelligence. It's an important intelligence trait. **Life and people in it want to be appreciated for what they give you, and they expect to get something in return, even if it's just a thank you.**

I have seen people, whom I consider very intelligent, fail because they lacked appreciation for life and the people around them. The rebellious child thinks that he is getting away with his behavior if his parents are not kicking him out of the house. He is not. He is missing out on a lot of opportunities for himself because his parents are busy defending themselves from him as opposed to looking out for ways to help him.

Anyone who thinks that life owes them something, sooner than later, will have a rude awakening. Life is based on exchange, when people do something for you they expect something in return, even if that something is a smile, a thank you, a pat on the back.

As a general rule the more you appreciate what life is giving you, the more life will give you back.

The word appreciate has two meanings:

1. Thank you.
2. To fully assess what people and life in general have offered or continue to offer you.

I tell my children definition #2 is the most important as they need to be fully aware of what it took (other people's hard work and meticulous thought process) for my children to get what they have. As a child, you might think that what you got from your parents or others is very mediocre, but do you really know what sacrifices they had to make in order for you to be able to receive that?

Anytime anyone does anything for you, see what they had to do based on their station in life, to provide that to you and thank them. Regardless, openly appreciate anything anyone does for your benefit. The minute you feel that others owe you, you are in trouble. **You can be proud of yourself all you want, but appreciate what you get from whomever you get it. Always!**

18. Willingness and Ability to Accept and Give Help Intelligence

Is this a form of intelligence? Absolutely! Smart people accept help and are willing to give help. The not so smart ones claim to be doing everything themselves. But ... who made their pants, their shirt, their car, their house, etc.?

Sit at a corner of a busy street and observe the faces of the people passing by. Do they look like they are part of a civilization giving and accepting help? I doubt it. Most look like they are in their own world and have no sense that the world is interwoven or that we are all heavily dependent on one another for survival.

Have you heard the phrase, "too proud to ask for help" or "he will not help anyone except himself"? People who feel either way are very disconnected from society and feel isolated. Their unwillingness to accept or give help isolates them, which lowers their survival potential greatly. Without the willingness to help and be helped the entire civilization is doomed to fail.

By the way, when people feel disconnected and are unwilling to help each other and do not work as a team is when they are most

vulnerable to becoming enslaved. More on that in the freedom intelligence traits coming up.

19. Trust and Allegiance Intelligence

When I was explaining to one of my family members that I was going to get a partner in one of my businesses she said: “Don’t trust anyone. They are all out for themselves.” When I asked why she felt this way, she went on to tell me about all the different people who *did her in*. However, I know of a lot of people who had helped this person greatly, yet in her criticisms, she declined to mention any of those who helped her.

As I discussed my prospective partnership further, she said: “Be smart, trust no one. I am smart and I don’t trust people, no matter what they say.” I was taken aback a bit by that and I asked: “Do you have any partnerships? Do you run any organizations? Are any people collaborating with you at present for mutual benefits?” To all these questions she answered no. Of course; she did not trust anyone as she was “too smart” to be fooled by people.

The easiest thing in the world is to trust no one, have no allegiance to any group and stay home for the day. But that gets you nowhere. The intelligent thing is to find the right people and collaborate with them for the benefit of all concerned.

I tell my staff: "I hired you, therefore I trust you. Although we live in the Midwest, if you told me there was an elephant outside, I would believe you. I would not bet my house on it, but I would believe you, and if it turned out to be otherwise that means you gave me a reason not to trust you. Until then, I trust you."

It takes a high level of intelligence and courage to trust people and try to collaborate with them for mutual benefit. Look around you; the more successful societies have developed a great deal of trust among each other and collaborate for the benefit of all. They have developed great companies, great universities, and great civic organizations, including churches. The less intelligent among us are lone wolves, working alone, trying to survive in some corner, fighting all others.

Trust and pledging allegiance to the right team for mutual benefit are necessary for your survival, let alone optimum survival.

To trust and work with people is a high degree of intelligence.

20. Inheritance or Cultural Intelligence

What you learn from your family, your immediate environment or culture can give you invaluable knowledge about life. Learn it well. This type of intelligence is very underestimated by people, but it makes a big difference for one's success in life.

The term self-made is overestimated by most. The taller the building, the deeper its foundation and no building stays up without a good foundation. **The foundation is our inherited knowledge.**

A few years back, I read a biography about Rupert Murdoch (the media mogul). The biography claimed that he is self-made and he singlehandedly created his media empire. However, it also stated that he was sent from Australia, where he was born, to study at the Oxford University in England and that when he completed his studies, he went back to Australia to work with his father from whom he inherited two newspapers, in two different Australian territories (states). The above sounds like a great deal of foundation to me, which was not made by Mr. Murdoch himself, but by others before him. Just the connections related to the media business alone were invaluable, let alone the know-how he got in publishing newspapers.

As a teenager, I was told that in America almost everyone is self-made and that after age eighteen, teenagers go off on their own either to college or to get a job. When I got to dental school, the average age of my freshman class was twenty-four and the majority of the students, I discovered, either lived at home or close to home and got some help from their parents. Undoubtedly, a lot of teenagers do go off on their own, but obviously not the ones who go on to professional school and beyond. So much for strictly self-made.

Certain groups, cultures or religious denominations are more successful than others. Why? It is because of the knowledge they possess and pass on to their members and their offspring who then inherit this type of intelligence.

What is your group's philosophy about life? What are their beliefs on helping each other? How do they handle other people? What are their beliefs about money and how do they handle money? All these traits you and your children inherit.

The groups that have useful knowledge and know-how about life have an advantage over other groups who don't possess any or much.

Hopefully your family or group contains a great deal of useful knowledge and know-hows about life. If not, seek a group that does.

21. Ability to be Part of a Winning Team Intelligence

Life is a game and games are played with teams. In order to win, you must have the best possible team. Your family is usually your most important team. Even if you are a loner, this team concept still applies as your team could be your family, your company, the university you are getting your education from, or could be your country as a whole. Tesla was a great inventor, far better than Edison in my opinion, yet he died relatively an unknown because his team was not as strong as Edison's.

Archimedes, the brightest mind of the ancient world, was failed by his team as they could not protect him from the enemies and he was killed by the Romans during a battle.

Which team do you join? It depends on your goals and what teams are available to you. A team must align with your philosophy about life, it must enhance it and therefore enhance your goals; otherwise, what is the point of joining that particular team? In a lot of people's minds any team is better than no team, but that is not true since a bad team can destroy you. So, don't compromise your integrity and your goals, find a team that aligns with both.

If your team is not winning, can you make them into winners? Any CEO, or president of any organization, must have the ability to create a winning team.

To be able to work with a team and be part of a winning team is a must in life in order to be successful. It is also more fun to be part of a team as opposed to be alone without one.

22. Affinity Intelligence

Affinity = 1. To desire, to like or admire something;

2. To attract something (see chemical bonds).

Affinity toward others and the world in general makes one happier and therefore more successful.

When Christ said: "Love thy neighbor," He was promoting this intelligence trait. The translation from the original Greek to English is poor. More accurately, He said: "Love each other." Said otherwise, "have affinity for other people or mankind in general." It has been proven that the larger your affinity for yourself, your family, your neighbors and the world is, the bigger your chances for success.

How is this different than, say, appreciation? Well, you can appreciate something for what it is and express thanks, but that does not mean you like it or that you have great affinity for it.

Love and sex are included in this intelligence trait, but these are only part of it. To have affinity for the world at large, you need to encompass other people besides your immediate environment. The most popular cultures in history have been the Hellenic (Greek) and American. Why? Because they exhibited the most affinity toward the world as they promoted individual freedom and democracy and they shared everything they discovered with the rest of the world.

People who have great affinity for the world tend to work the hardest, create great things and are happier people. It is probably the opposite of what you get from television, but isn't that so for most things? Television portrays the bums at the beach as fun-loving individuals who love the world and the scrooge who works day and night as hating the world. Look closer. It might not be so. Perhaps the bum at the beach has very little affinity toward anything else, especially a job, therefore he ends up at the beach or at the local pub to get away from it all.

We all have arms.
The difference is on
how we use them.
Most people use them to
hug themselves;
others to hug the neighborhood.
A few use them to hug the world.

As I was finishing this book I got my hands on a letter sent by Einstein to his daughter, Lieserl. He describes a similar concept so I enclose it here fully.

A letter from Albert Einstein to his daughter: about The Universal Force, which is LOVE

April 15, 2015 Ines Redman Uncategorized Albert Einstein, love

In the late 1980s, Lieserl, the daughter of the famous genius, donated 1,400 letters, written by Einstein, to the Hebrew University, with orders not to publish their contents until two decades after his death. This is one of them, for Lieserl Einstein.

…" When I proposed the theory of relativity, very few understood me, and what I will reveal now to transmit to mankind will also collide with the misunderstanding and prejudice in the world.
I ask you to guard the letters as long as necessary, years, decades, until society is advanced enough to accept what I will explain below.
There is an extremely powerful force that, so far, science has not found a formal explanation to. It is a force that includes and governs all others, and is even behind any phenomenon operating in the universe and has not yet been identified by us.

This universal force is LOVE.
When scientists looked for a unified theory of the universe they forgot the most powerful unseen force.

Love is Light, that enlightens those who give and receive it.
Love is gravity, because it makes some people feel attracted to others.

Love is power, because it multiplies the best we have, and allows humanity not to be extinguished in their blind selfishness. Love unfolds and reveals.

For love we live and die.
Love is God and God is Love.

This force explains everything and gives meaning to life. This is the variable that we have ignored for too long, maybe because we are afraid of love because it is the only energy in the universe that man has not learned to drive at will.

To give visibility to love, I made a simple substitution in my most famous equation.

If instead of E = mc2, we accept that the energy to heal the world can be obtained through love multiplied by the speed of light squared, we arrive at the conclusion that love is the most powerful force there is, because it has no limits.
After the failure of humanity in the use and control of the other forces of the universe that have turned against us, it is urgent that we nourish ourselves with another kind of energy…

If we want our species to survive, if we are to find meaning in life, if we want to save the world and every sentient being that inhabits it, love is the one and only answer.
Perhaps we are not yet ready to make a bomb of love, a device powerful enough to entirely destroy the hate, selfishness and greed that devastate the planet.

However, each individual carries within them a small but powerful generator of love whose energy is waiting to be released.
When we learn to give and receive this universal energy, dear Lieserl, we will have affirmed that love conquers all, is able to

transcend everything and anything, because love is the quintessence of life.

I deeply regret not having been able to express what is in my heart, which has quietly beaten for you all my life. Maybe it's too late to apologize, but as time is relative, I need to tell you that I love you and thanks to you I have reached the ultimate answer!

Your father Albert Einstein

Chapter F

Ethics Intelligence

23. Ethics Intelligence

The word ethics comes from the Greek word Hθος (ethos) which means the character or quality of something. So ethics signifies the quality of a being. It's the most important quality of the human spirit; without it we are just animals and out of control. Fairness is part of ethics. Without a sense of fairness, no culture can endure.

When I hire someone, the most important quality I look for is his/her ethics level. The first question I ask myself about any prospective employee is: Can I trust this person? Will he be an ally in our endeavor or will he turn out to be an enemy? Why would I want someone in my company who is not ethical? If this person is in a high enough position, he will destroy my company sooner than later.

Ethics does not mean to keep your nose clean or to be a good boy or a good girl.

Success in life is ethical.
Failure is unethical.

It means possessing the right ethos, the right character to obtain optimum survival.

Therefore, something that is not helping toward optimum survival is not ethical. Staying home, instead of going to work to earn a living to provide for your family, is not ethical. Having a good ethos and a sense of fairness is paramount to survival. Ethical and fair- minded people survive as they are supported by others. Unethical people do not survive, at least not for long. Look at history. Also, despite what some people assert, a low ethics person is despised and not trusted by anyone, even the ones who use such a person.

In our society today, the best index of ethics is the treatment of money. Money represents condensed energy, condensed labor. Where do people put their condensed sweat for safekeeping? Wherever they trust that it will be treated most fairly and ethically and even with reverence. Globally speaking, at this time money flows mostly toward the capitals of the Western World as people feel that it will be treated most fairly there. For that reason, places like London and New York get money coming to them from all over the world that contributes to their wealth.

Show me a country that mishandles earned labor and I will show you an unethical and poor country. The idea of government confiscating bank deposits is perverse and it breaks down the fabric of society in more ways than people realize. Also, debasing or destroying a country's currency creates chaos and even civil unrest.

All people are capable of creating things. If people's efforts are not rewarded or they feel that they are not treated fairly, then people will just stop trying altogether and the culture disintegrates.

Ethics is a quality all people have to some degree, even the ones who pretend that they don't.

The two basic rules of ethical conduct in everyday life are:

a. Treat others as you would want to be treated, if you were in their situation.
b. Do what you promised to do.

24. Justice and Fairness Intelligence

Justice is related to ethics, but someone may be very ethical on his own accord, but not intelligent enough to handle justice. Justice is the handling of people who have gone astray in terms of their ethical conduct. As a leader of a group, you will constantly be asked to handle justice actions. How well you handle them has to do with your overall intelligence on this subject.

For example: Your employee Frank called Joe (his coworker) "an elephant," an unethical behavior, and now Joe is mad at Frank. You are asked to handle the dispute between Frank and Joe. How well you handle this depends on your justice and fairness intelligence. If it's a good result, you are intelligent in this area; if not, you lack this type of intelligence.

Nothing upsets people more than the feeling that they were treated unfairly. When handling justice, you need to be able to do the right thing for the circumstances and for the people involved.

Fairness among groups also means getting a decent chance. If people feel that they got a fair chance they seem to be okay with the outcome, even if they failed; but if they perceive that they were treated unfairly compared to others then they will feel bitter. Civil unrest comes about when different groups feel that they are treated unfairly or that they did not get a fair chance.

Notice I said fair, not equal. The struggle to give its members a fair chance is a constant struggle for any society rich or poor. But they must try in order to keep the society intact. It is constant because no people or groups are ever truly equal. We are all created with different talents and abilities in various grades and levels. That is why the free enterprise system is the only system that provides the best fairness index. For more on that read my book *Political Systems and Their Relationship to Economics and Freedom.*

In handling justice, the most important rules are the following:

1. Always use as a guide the two basic rules of ethical conduct, which are:
    a. Treat others as you would want to be treated, if you were in their situation.
    b. Do what you promised to do.
2. The punishment must fit the crime and justice should not be vindictive.
3. The result should improve society and not harm it.

4. The result should improve the individual, but not to the detriment of society.
5. Insanity is not a defense. Judge on what was actually done. Of course, the serial killer was insane, but he took the lives of many innocent people and created havoc for many others.
6. Don't make an example of someone with excessive punishment. See rule #2.
7. All laws and government policies should be simple enough to be understood by all citizens and should be taught to all concerned constantly.
8. Constantly try to make sure that all concerned citizens fully know the consequences of breaking the law and these consequences should follow the above points.

These apply to a family, a school, or any organization big or small as well as a country.

You cannot be any kind of a leader without justice and fairness intelligence.

25. Ability to Discriminate Intelligence

Not all people you come in contact with are good for you. Also, all careers are not the same. Each association and each career path have very different outcomes. So, which career path do you follow? Which group will you befriend? You must discriminate among people and career paths and make the proper choices. Keeping the wrong people around you will be detrimental to you, and your ability to reach your goals will be greatly diminished. Spending time on things that are not propelling you toward your goals will also be detrimental to you.

It has been said that hard work pays great dividends. I would rephrase this to state: **Hard work in the right endeavor and with the right companions pays great dividends.**

A *master's degree in gang membership* might take many years to obtain as you are hanging around the wrong people, but society might not have much use for it and might not want to pay you for such knowledge at all (assuming you come out alive).

As a different example, you can be a highly paid executive, but with the wrong spouse by your side, you can end up in poverty and with poor health. I have seen what I would call brilliant people marry the wrong person and end up miserable and not so brilliant.

So, not all roads lead to Rome. Be intelligent and choose the right road and the right companions.

26. The Ability to Overcome Your Ego Intelligence

The word ego comes from the Greek word *εγω (ego)*, which means I or me. In modern terms, it is used with the idea of excessive self-pride such as in the word: egotistical.

Although it is good to have self-pride and to believe in yourself, it is detrimental to cater to your own ego in a manner that disregards any consequences.

In life, we constantly have to handle things and people and we are asked to decide one way or the other. To be successful individually and as a group you need to determine in each occasion what is the desired outcome for all concerned under the circumstances and not just serve your ego.

To do the right thing under the circumstances involves putting your ego aside and to have thought a predetermined outcome before you embark on handling something or someone. As an example, when I walk into a room for a meeting with a staff member, I need to have thought out beforehand what I expect out of this meeting, otherwise I am rolling the dice. Perhaps this staff member committed an offense against the office and I am asked to handle it. But, before I go into the meeting, I must project the outcome that I want out of this handling and steer the meeting toward that direction. As such, I think the communication through and figure out what I need to say to correct the staff member and still keep him on the team if that is what I want. Otherwise, if I just walk into a meeting and accuse someone of an offense and just defend my position, I will automatically make the other person wrong. He might then spin and run out crying and quit simply because I bruised his ego. If that is not the outcome I want, I need to think things through ahead of time and steer the meeting carefully toward the desired outcome.

By the way, if you want to get rid of a staff member just bruise his/her ego and they are gone.

This ego thing also goes along with holding grudges and never wanting to give in. **The teachings of Christ about forgiving is using this type of intelligence.** I am not sure that you need to forgive a terrible, purposeful misdeed, but I know that holding on to grudges does one no good. Part of what helped me with this is the understanding that people are not as able or as intelligent as they appear. Most misdeeds in life are caused by lack of intelligence. The person just couldn't figure out a better solution; he was not that intelligent. So don't be unintelligent yourself, do the right thing to get the most optimum result and not what your ego cries out for.

This applies to many aspects of life, especially communication. During all communications with people it is important to convey the information that causes the right outcome for all concerned and not a perverted communication that causes harm by bruising people's egos. For example, your coworker does not need to know what another coworker said about her exactly in the heat of anger; **you must deliver a truthful message**, but one that works for everyone's benefit and not to hurt someone or destroy the harmony of the group. You can leave out of the communication details that hurt people and are not necessary to convey.

I have seen many able people who have a tremendously strong need to be right even when they are wrong, and this flaw leads them to failure. Just recently I was helping a young person with a college application and I reviewed an essay he wrote of which he was very proud. Nevertheless, I thought his essay did not put him in the best possible light as he did not put down several attributes he had. So, I revised the essay greatly. The student was puzzled about my revision and said he would go over these with his counselor. I said: "That's a good idea, show him both essays (my revision and his original) and see what he thinks." He agreed. The next communication I got from the student was that his counselor thought his essay was good enough and he was happy about what his counselor had said about it. Later I found out that he never showed his counselor my revised version. I guess it was more important for him to be right about his essay than making sure he got the best possible chance to be accepted by that particular university.

By the way, do you know what the #1 reason is that people start their own business? It is to exalt their own ego. How do I know that? I have a consulting company that helps small businesses and in that endeavor, I discovered that the majority of people want to be right in what they are doing even if it is not working and not look at another viewpoint on how to run their business.

The more intelligent one is, the more he can put aside his ego and do the right thing.
This is a divine ability very few people possess.

If you have goals you are trying to reach, you can see how the above is helpful, useful, and easy to follow. If you have no goals in life, then your ego overcomes you and gets the best of you, and exulting your ego becomes your only game.

Chapter G

Awareness Intelligence

27. Awareness Intelligence

Awareness is the ability to understand the scene around you. It is the duplication of how people and objects around one are arranged and how they influence each other. It is the understanding of the past and the ability to perceive the future. The sixth sense would be included in this type of intelligence.

Some people walk past a gruesome accident and don't even see it. Others seem to *smell* the accident a mile away. One is able to pick up the vibe that Tom Jones does not like him, while another seems oblivious to it.

In the 1930s many political leaders around the world felt that Hitler was a reasonable man they could negotiate with. Winston Churchill felt otherwise. In the 1940s those leaders realized that they were wrong, but by then it was too late. At the same time, some very aware Jews in Germany sensed that bad things were coming and left the country; others were convinced that the good German people who were dressed in Nazi uniforms posed no real danger to them or their families.

Do you ever suspect that if a certain person or an organization had absolute power over you, they might try to overwhelm you? Some people don't even suspect that.

Do you ever think that the people who are feeding you information via books and media could have agendas and that they might not be as fair-minded as they appear? Do you understand why the American forefathers put checks and balances in our political and economic system and the right to bear arms?[5]

All the above have to do with the awareness intelligence.

[5] Arms: Anything that can be used as protection. Military weaponry can be a part of it, but arms do not necessarily equal weapons. Protection today is done mostly via media, supporting the pro-freedom politicians and legal means.

28. Ability to Confront Intelligence

Confront: To see and accept something for what it is without distorting what one sees by wishing it was different than it is.

Do you accept what you see in life? Do you understand it fully or do you brush things off and pretend that things are different than what they really are?

The one quality that all good executives have in common is their willingness and ability to confront and thereafter handle whatever they face in their organization or life. If you can't confront something for what it is, how can you possibly begin to handle or fix it? You can't.

Confront = the basic to handling anything.

Confront = Honesty = Sanity.

Honesty to yourself is the foundation to your life. A lot of people are not honest and therefore lie to themselves about things they have to deal with in life because they are unable to confront them. I have acquaintances who pretend to be something totally different than who they really are. They think they are fooling everybody. At the end, they only fool themselves.

The inability to see things for what they are is probably the most dangerous of all human frailties. Starting to handle something in life without fully confronting it, and therefore not understanding its importance or unimportance as it relates to other things, is like trying to traverse an ocean without navigation devices. Confront is the compass of life. It tells you where north is and without it who knows where you will end up. I certainly wouldn't want to be on your ship.

The ability and willingness to see and accept life and things around one as they truly are, is the most basic of all the intelligence traits.

29. Observation Intelligence

This is the ability to see all there is to see in any given situation.

This is similar to the awareness intelligence, but different in the sense that one observes exactly what is there. In terms of awareness, one may be aware of a danger coming, but might not be able to understand and analyze fully where it is coming from and why. Whereas, another who has heightened observation ability and knows more about the subject can see exactly what there is to see in regard to this subject or situation involved.

For example, before I became a dentist, when I would look at people's teeth, I had awareness about them. I could tell if they were pretty or not or if they had dental problems, but I did not have a full observational ability about them. After I became a dentist I gained a heightened observational ability in anything that had to do with teeth. I can now see people's teeth exactly as they are in full detail; I can see if they have an excessive overjet, overbite, Type III occlusion, if they are chipped or bonded, whether the person has a reverse smile line, an off midline, a peg lateral, etc. I can fully observe everything there is to be observed in one's mouth in no time at all.

Therefore, this intelligence trait is enhanced greatly by experience and the secondhand knowledge intelligence.

One must be able to observe in order to gain knowledge about a subject. But of course, he must first be able to confront what one is observing.

30. Proper Estimation of Effort Intelligence

What does it really take to complete a job, a college degree, or to succeed in a particular business endeavor? The majority of people cannot properly estimate what it really takes to do a task or bring some job to fruition.

In order to succeed in life, it is paramount to be able to estimate the necessary effort needed for anything you are interested in pursuing.

Imagine an army commander who is charging to take a hill, but has not realized and therefore not taken into consideration that his tanks will not be able to climb easily due to heavy gravel found on that hill. He will fall short of his efforts and will be defeated.

In your everyday efforts, have you noticed at times how the day has gone by, yet you have only accomplished a fraction of what you planned on doing for that day? It is because it usually takes a lot more effort to do things than one originally predicts. This is true with everything in life, such as in studying for an exam, learning a new skill, starting a business, etc.

Successful people know this fact well, so they plan well and spend a lot more time and energy on projects than others. They properly estimate the necessary effort needed and muster the necessary energy and resources to accomplish the goals they set out for themselves. That is one of the main reasons they are successful.

31. The Ability to Perceive the Sequence or Consequences Intelligence

The main reason people do stupid things in life is because they lack this intelligence trait. They do things reactively without realizing the consequences afterwards. They cannot visualize the sequence of events that will follow and how it will affect them.

It would be good for our society if children at school were shown actual illegal or immoral acts or even just dumb actions documented on video or otherwise and the consequences that unfolded afterwards. For instance, show them an incident where a child robbed a store and how later the child was caught and after he was convicted in court, spent five years in jail, which scarred him for life and put him five years behind with all that it entails. On a different example, show how a diving escapade in dark and unknown waters paralyzed someone for life, or something similar, but you get the idea.

The main reason I never picked up smoking was because I would remember vividly how it felt the day after smoking. My clothes smelled bad and my throat felt terrible. So when I was offered a cigarette at a party I would not take it, visualizing the unpleasant consequences the day after.

As another example, having an extramarital affair might feel exciting now, but can you walk it through in your mind and follow the consequences? Perhaps then you will reconsider.

In a geopolitical sense let's say the nearby king upset you because he threw a fish. You feel like going to war with him to teach him a lesson. You reckon he is ugly anyway and rearranging his face would probably be better for his looks. So you think: "Let's go to war and have a brawl". But wait, let's have a look at the consequences to our people and all concerned. Let's walk it through mentally and plot a few scenarios. Now, do you still think it is a good idea to go and have a brawl with this ugly king?

It is equally important if one can carry the sequence for an incident or a situation backward as well and see exactly what was caused and by whom, in order to place the proper credit or blame on the right person or group for a particular outcome. As an example, let's say one is boasting about his good position in life and how well he is doing; but can he follow the sequence backward and discover who and what was truly responsible for his good fortune? If he did that, then he can know with certainty who is responsible for his success in an endeavor and give this person or group the proper appreciation.

If one can't do that then he will not know how he got here and therefore cannot maintain this successful action in the future.

All the above exemplify the ability to string out, if you will, and observe the possible sequences and consequences going forward and backward and see how things unfolded in the past or how they might unfold in the future and why. You can easily see how this is a great intelligence trait one needs in order to succeed in life.

Chapter H

Leadership Intelligence

32. Leadership Intelligence

It takes a certain type of intelligence to be able **to lead** a family, a team or an organization. I call it Leadership Intelligence. **This part of intelligence very few people possess, yet it is the most important ability for any kind of success by a group or a society.**

If you ask one hundred people if they wanted a leadership role in their job, half would say yes, but when confronted with the task, only 10% or less will take it. Even this 10% will be proven that it possesses very little true leadership capabilities and when in charge they will have a tendency to blame others for their team's failure.

True leaders, who can take a group to a destination, are very few in this world.

A true leader must be wise, which means he must possess most of the traits of intelligence described in this book. He must definitely possess justice intelligence, great communication skills, courageous positivity, perseverance, social intelligence, and the application intelligence.

The leader of any group is the driver of that group or activity. Any operation, be it a business, a church or any type of organization, needs a leader at the very top and in each department to **drive it**! A true leader is the **DRIVER** of the group or the organization and it is up to him if the group ends up at its destination. This driver has the entire responsibility for the success of the organization or the division on his shoulders to run it daily, monthly, yearly, and beyond.

In life things either go up or down, they either grow or shrink; nothing stays the same. This is also true for an organization, even a physical structure such as a building; it is either improving or getting worse. **But, in order for an organization to grow, there has to be a leader present to make it grow.** He is the *rainmaker* who *makes rain* for the *crops to be watered* and makes sure that things will continue to grow.

The idea of someone being in charge of a company and vacationing permanently in the Bahamas is false. It does not work that way. If you want to move away, then assign someone else to be the leader or driver of the company or the organization with full control and full responsibility.

Any organization is composed of different parts. At different times these parts need to be fixed or replaced or just altered, and its leaders or drivers must be there to constantly do just that.

An executive, any executive in an organization, is the leader of his division or area. What does the word executive mean? It comes from the word executor.

Webster's New World College Dictionary, Fourth Edition, states the derivation of executor comes from "ME executor < L Executus: to follow up, pursue < sequie, to follow: a person who gets something done or produced."

It comes from two words: Ex and Sequie (sequence)

Taking this further back to two Greek words.

EX< ΕΞΩ = Exterior and Sequie < ΣΕΙΡΑ = Line or sequence

In my opinion, an executive literally means the one outside the sequence or line. Therefore, executive or leader is the person who is outside the line of work or the sequence of work (the assembly line).

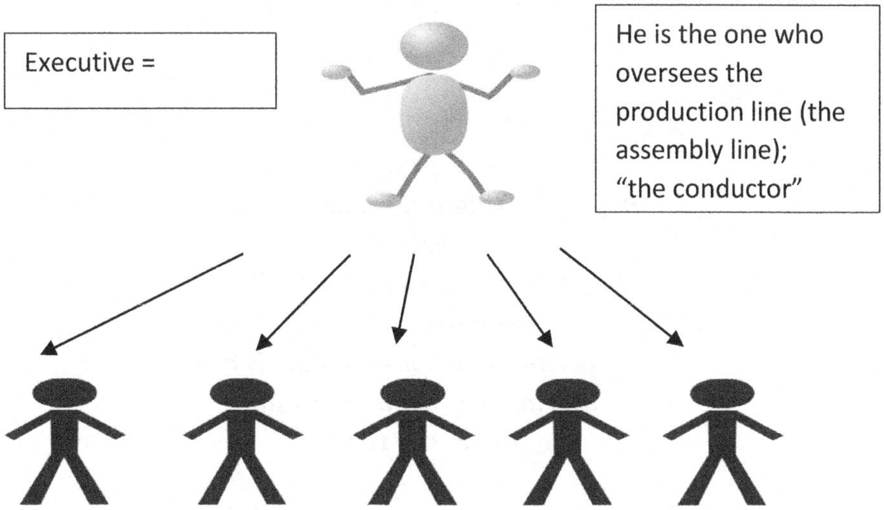
Executive =
He is the one who oversees the production line (the assembly line); "the conductor"

Line of people doing the work or the sequence line or the production line.

Execute: to act as an executive. It is a verb. It describes an action. It describes activity. It is constant alertness and constant action.

Although there is a constant flux in any organization, its leader must not waver, never get tired, nor have any personal issues, and his ethics must be beyond reproach. He is superhuman. He is relentless and drives the machine faster than anyone can catch up to it. Everyone is barely hanging on to their job and constantly getting trained to the new demands the leader puts on with expansion in mind for the benefit of the people it serves; customers, employees, and owners. Further, the leader makes everyone feel that the organization will continue to run to eternity.

In leading a group, the most important things a leader must do are:

(a) to set a destination for the group to reach, and

(b) specific goals for each member to accomplish within a certain amount of time.

33. Causative Intelligence

To be cause = the ability to cause something small or big and in general, one's ability to control his environment. The opposite of cause is effect.

What is cause? What is effect?

Cause is the point of emanation of energy toward something else. Control is also a factor.

For example: the light bulb emanates energy in the room and therefore it is cause over lighting of the room. Of course, the guy who put the lightbulb there in the first place is the real cause over the entire subject of lighting the room.

Another example: A sergeant in the army is in charge of his unit so he is cause over his soldiers.

Cause has many gradients. One can be cause over his family or he can be cause over an entire country. These are two very different cause levels. The mechanic who knows little about engines can be a little causative over engines. The mechanic who is at the top of his field can be very causative over engines.

Effect is the exact opposite of cause.

When I think of effect, a flower garden comes to mind. It waits there patiently to be watered. If no one walks over to water them, the flowers die. If someone decides to pull or cut the flowers from the garden, the flowers just sit there and accept it.

We can plot the concept of cause and effect on a linear line as seen below.

On one extreme you would have a pebble that can be kicked by anyone and on the other extreme you would have a superstar.

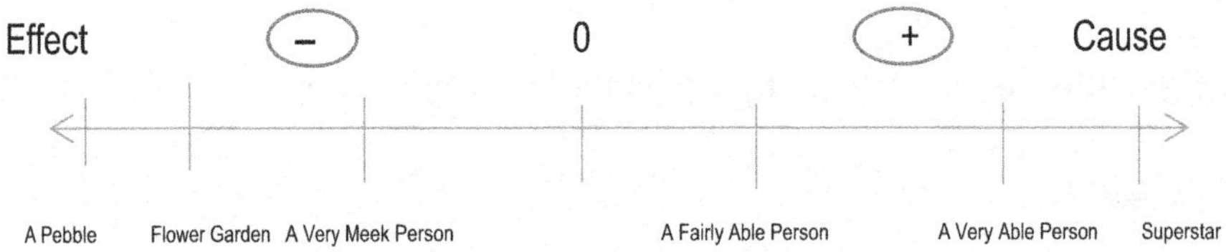

Therefore, cause and effect come at all levels in business and in life.

Do you want to create things in your life and business? Then you need to be causative. You need to make things happen. An entire book can be written on this subject as people today are trained not to be cause but effect.

Assignment of Cause: Assignment of cause is the most important aspect of the subject. For example, if someone has you down on the floor and is stepping on your neck, you can assign cause to him as it seems obvious, or you can assign cause to yourself saying: "What did I do to be in this situation?" By doing the latter, you can be cause and decide to do something about it, as opposed to claim to be the effect and do nothing and continue to be the effect forever and ever.

How causative are you, in life? Do you take responsibility for your life or are you waiting for others to "water" you?

As a fun example, say you spot a beautiful girl at a party. Can you be causative and walk over and talk to her? If so, you might have a happy life. If not, well . . .

First and foremost, you need to want to be cause over your environment or job, which will lead you to gain the necessary knowledge in order to be cause over them.

Knowledge, ability, and the willingness to use them would make someone more cause.

True leaders are by definition causative.

34. Capacity Intelligence

How much load can you handle in your life? Some people can handle a country, others can barely handle their own household. A true leader must have a high capacity intelligence.

Elon Musk came to the United States from another country and took on the entire motor industry with his company Tesla. At the same time NASA is giving his other company, Space X, billions to develop rockets. Elon Musk possesses great capacity intelligence. Others can barely confront the purchase of a small house and ponder on it for years.

The ability to be able to fire on multiple cylinders at once is a form of intelligence. How many cylinders can you fire on simultaneously?

Great capacity intelligence does not necessarily mean the ability to make money. Walt Disney had great capacity intelligence and could think globally, but he was not good at making money. J.P Morgan on the other hand, had both abilities; he was able to handle many big ventures at once and was able to make money from doing them.

Any CEO worth his salt or a president of a country must possess this type of intelligence in spades, otherwise he will stop most of the incoming barrage of information and certainly will avoid doing all the things that need to be done for this high-level job.

35. Courageous Positivity Intelligence

It is the ability to have the courage to be positive about life and the outcome of things and the ability to exude that positivity on others and encourage them to do well.

A leader must possess the ability to be positive and courageous about life and people despite reasons to be pessimistic and scared. This ability affects people in a positive manner and propels them toward better survival as opposed to succumb.

The people who exude courageous positivity are the ones you look forward to seeing because they bring you hope and warm feelings. We all need people like that to get us through the day, the week, or the month. If people around you do not exude courageous positivity, at least most of the time, they are shackles on your feet. The worst part about it is that you might not even notice them, as people who are negative about life try to disguise their glumness[6] by trying to convince you that it's not them weighing you down, but rather that life is hard and limiting.

Life on planet Earth can be hard for all of us. Do you have the courage and fortitude to be positive about life for yourself and others

---

[6] Glumness: gloominess

around you despite hard times? If so, you are an invaluable ally, an invaluable friend. **Life could not be livable without people who possess courageous positivity.**

This type of intelligence has less to do with how one feels and more to do with how he exudes positivity to others. This is an ability any leader of any group (large or small) must possess. He must believe that there is light at the end of the tunnel and that he will find it. Also, he must believe in his abilities to create a light as necessary, if one is not found, so that his group can use it and find their way out of the tunnel. Otherwise, why should people follow and assign him to be their leader?

36. Seize the Moment Intelligence

Let's say you have specific goals and have outlined a clear path to reach them, but as you are working toward these goals something happens, an opportunity or a crisis. Do you jump and seize the moment or does fear and inertia cause you to do nothing? Most people are so busy with their everyday lives that if someone told them there was a bucket of gold buried in their back yard and that it will take a couple of days to dig it up, they will say they are too busy for the task.

Bill Gates was a student at Harvard, one of the most prestigious universities. Yet when the opportunity arose, which he perceived fully, he dropped out of Harvard and seized the moment. Bill Gates had the intelligence to perceive and seize the opportunity to develop Microsoft.

Who would have blamed Bill Gates if he had stayed at Harvard and finished college? Today he would have been a very successful professional in any area he pursued and I am sure he would have been a multimillionaire. Most likely though, not a multibillionaire or a leader of a global behemoth. A billionaire is 1,000 times richer than a millionaire. Yes, one thousand times! That is what happens when you seize the right opportunity. The difference between seizing it and not is astronomical.

It is the same concept when you prevent a disaster. Doing something to handle a crisis could mean the difference between life and death for you, your group, or nation.

So, *carpe diem* (seize the day) and propel yourself to a higher plateau of survival and or greatness.

There is a risk in jumping out of one's comfort zone to seize a perceived opportunity, but there is no greatness without this intelligence trait.

---

37. Urgency Intelligence

You have seized the moment and embarked on a given course of action to develop an opportunity or to prevent a calamity. Well done! But, seizing the moment or jumping on the opportunity is only the first step, although a major one; now you need to make this into a total victory.

You need to create a sense of urgency for yourself and your people to move fast enough to develop the product or service and make it before you run out of resources or the competition outruns you.

You seized the enemy's intelligence data and know his moves. Can you move fast enough to surprise him and overwhelm him or will you be too slow to make this into a total victory?

I tell my children that school will be over soon and that their grades will be engraved in stone. There is only so much time and then it is over.

Most people are fearful of the unknown and as inertia (doing the same thing over and over) sets in they get too comfortable. If you perceive an opportunity or a calamity, and you are attempting to capitalize on the opportunity or handle the calamity, you must create a sense of urgency in others. Without this urgency, people will not move fast enough for the occasion.

As a leader, you need to create a sense of urgency in your team's minds and not allow them to get sidetracked or lax.

Without this sense of urgency, you will not be able to develop the operation into a fruitful endeavor, and it will be a too little too late type of thing.

As a general rule, people around you are busy with mundane, everyday stuff and enjoy being busy. By creating a sense of urgency, you push people past these mundane issues and/or everyday problems and get them to focus on the goals and the products envisioned.

By the way, the best way for any one of us to handle our everyday problems is to create urgency and focus on big long-term goals. When you emphasize the goals and are busy pursuing them, most everyday problems will just drop out.

Urgency toward your goals is the best way
to handle your everyday problems;
they will just cease to exist.

---

38. Daring Intelligence

This is similar to the ability to seize the moment, but different in the sense that this has to do with everyday life and not necessarily with a single big opportunity or a major crisis.

The ancient Greeks had a saying: "The daring one wins."

Most people are so afraid, they can't even dare to ask someone out on a date, let alone dare to do a business venture or speak out about an injustice. They would rather be wrong than alone but that is not the winning man's recipe.

Do you dare to walk up to a prospective customer and give them your card? Do you dare to be responsible for your immediate and distant environment? If you don't agree with something that is happening around you do you dare to fix it?

The proper word is dare. Dare to win, dare to speak up, dare to start something. Dare to be politically active. Dare to be responsible. Dare to say no to your friends about things they are doing that are inappropriate, because if you don't, it is assumed that you are condoning their behavior.

Only the daring ones affect the world. They are the ones who are moving the wheel of life. The rest just live on the spokes of the wheel, thinking mistakenly, that they are also pushing it along.

A popular song says "Born to be wild." You don't have to be wild. You just have to dare and act. But, I guess that is wild during these times of little responsibility by most.

39. Ability to Follow the Proper Leader Intelligence

Most intelligent people want to do things their way, which is a good quality to have as one forges toward a new product, a new concept, or a new system he is developing.

However, no one will ever know everything in life . . . not by a long shot. **Therefore, for one to succeed, he must find the proper mentors, i.e., successful people who have done the things one aspires to do, in order for him to be able to leapfrog ahead and be a huge success.**

Howard Hughes was one of the richest and most eccentric personalities in American history. Yet it has been said that if he just followed in the footsteps of his inheritances from his family, he would have ended better off financially without going through all the tumultuousness he had to endure. When I learned that I was amazed. I guess he wanted to do things his way.

To find and follow great mentors or leaders is truly a great intelligence trait despite the belief to the contrary. In fact this trait could possibly be the most important intelligence trait for the

majority of people. Why? Because the majority of us are not interested in owning our own business or developing and/or running our own organizations. Running a business is a different animal than being a great performer in an art or a profession, which is what most people desire. Therefore, the majority of people will go through life working for a company owned by someone else and will most likely follow a leader in that organization or business. As such, one's ability to pick the right leader or the right boss, if you will, could perhaps be the most important thing that he does, at least in terms of his career.

This is not as easy a task as you might think. Mentorship and advice are like medicine, in that if it is given by the right doctor who knows what to give you and in the right doses, it can save your life. If it's given by someone who does not know what the proper medicine for you is, or it is given in the wrong doses, it will kill you. Great leaders lead their people to the Promised Land; bad leaders lead their people to the guillotine or to the Siberian Mountains.

Your ability to pick the right leader, mentor, boss, could mean the difference between life and death, so pick wisely!

40. Judgment Intelligence

Given all the facts and all the information available about a subject, can you make a good judgment that will lead you toward the best possible solution for the issue or the problem at hand? As we go through life, we constantly have to judge people and circumstances and decide based on the information available to us at that time. Are you a good judge of people's character? Can you correctly judge a book? Can you pick the best leader? The best teammates? When you come to the fork at the end of the road, do you take the best route for you considering your circumstances or do you make the wrong decision and take the one that leads to the swamp?

Some people can be lied to, others not so easily. Given the same data, one person sees flaws with what was deduced from them; others do not see any problems with the conclusions drawn.

This intelligence trait does not exist in the absence of the ability to think for yourself. If you would rather be wrong than alone, you will not have good judgment intelligence.

In one of my classes in grammar school they showed us a film on how petroleum was made. Subsequently, we had to write an essay with the title "How was petroleum created?" I told the teacher that it seemed simplistic and I did not agree that petroleum could be made by dead plants and animals since it was found in different pockets around the world. I asked if that meant that only those areas had vegetation and dead dinosaurs. She laughed at me. Today the theory of petroleum being created from dead plants and dead animals has come into question.

On a similar concept, we are told that CO2 particles in the air will cause heat to be trapped inside the atmosphere. But can an argument be made that since these are actual particles they will also reflect the sun's rays and cause cooling instead?

The more you possess all the other intelligence traits, the better your judgement ability, assuming you are willing to confront what you see and know. The importance of Judgment Ability is second only to the Application Ability as you will discover later on in this book.

41. The Ability to Handle Power Intelligence

To be in a power position over others, means to serve people in a certain capacity and to be responsible to lead them toward a certain path with a clear direction in mind. Leading people in battle would be the ultimate responsibility for a power position.

A lot of people think that, to be the boss, or said otherwise, to have power over others, means to order people around at whim, and that they will just follow just because one is the boss. This is not the case at all. People are peculiar; the minute they perceive you are abusing your power or not using it properly they will oppose you, overtly or covertly.

Most people, when they get into a power position, start acting all weird or crazy. They lose touch with others and start living in an Ivory Tower and lose perspective. As such, they believe that the power position they find themselves in, is their right, and that they will never fall from it regardless of what they do. I know people, who grew up poor and due to hard work, great luck, or good connections, gained powerful positions but ended up losing them. Partly due to arrogance, but most due to lack of the knowledge and the ability to handle the power position they found themselves in; which they could have used to climb to even greater heights, but instead they fell from grace.

What happens to you when you go into a power position? Can you handle it well? Can you learn from the predecessors in that position? Or do you mishandle the state of power and lose it? Power is a hot seat and all eyes are on you. Any mistakes are magnified by several times by the people it affects. History is full of people who could have, but didn't, to the detriment to themselves and to the ones under them.

When in power, besides knowing how to handle it, one must also know when and to whom to pass it on to. George Washington according to history was offered to be king but declined it, for his benefit, as he went on to become an American Hero and a very wealthy man and to America's benefit as he established a democracy instead of a kingdom.

Others, especially military generals, who freed their countries from oppression have passed power prematurely to questionable politicians, to their detriment and the country's as well. How about patriarchs passing power prematurely to their offspring who end up destroying what they created?

Perhaps, the most important thing about power one must understand is that, it's not a forever type of thing once you acquire it. A power position to many seems like a very stable spot and no need to reinvent themselves. Nothing could be further from the truth. The position of Power is a constant balancing act, in order to be able to maintain it. The ancient Greek philosopher Heracletos said "ta panta rei," which means Everything Constantly Flows, or said otherwise everything is in constant change or flux; Same is true for power, nothing stays the same, you need to constantly do things in that position in order to stay in power. What must you do exactly? Increase your overall intelligence ability to handle the position of power. If you don't, you probably will never get into such position in the first place.

Chapter I

Planning and Organizational Intelligence

42. Organizational Intelligence

One of my classmates in college was extremely book smart. He did great at school without much stress it seemed, but if you walked into his room it looked like a hand grenade had just exploded. I would never want to go in a business partnership with him and if I had to, I would make sure that he was not involved in running the business. He would only be a dentist producing dentistry, but the business process would be organized by others.

If you own a business that is unorganized you will not know how much of a particular item you sold and what items you need to reorder. If your accounts are also unorganized you will not know if you are profiting or losing money.

Organization comes from the Greek word οργανο = organ, meaning a part of something with a specific function.

The opposite of organization is chaos, which comes from the Greek word χασμα (chasm) meaning a separation or a disconnection.

Therefore, organization literally means a working system of things (organs) as opposed to chaos or chasm. As an example, the body is an organization or a system of organs. It has a mouth used to chew food and an esophagus used for the transport of the food to the stomach where it breaks it down further and it then moves it throughout to nourish the body, which is what food is supposed to do. If we had a chaos or chasm, which is a void or a separation, such as a missing esophagus, then the food could not go from the mouth to the stomach; and despite the fact that the other organs, the mouth and stomach were working perfectly, the food could not be transported to the stomach and be utilized by the body, resulting in the death of the body.

So, to organize means to develop precise systems (organs) that work well together (are aligned properly) to develop and process the products and/or services one is producing.

The opposite of that would be a chaos (a separation in the process) and therefore lack of organization, resulting in the death of the company and or the suffering of the people involved.

Organization is key to success. John D. Rockefeller, a financial genius, was a stickler for organization as he documented and categorized all his business dealings very meticulously.

IBM had a saying: "Success is a system. Follow the system to success." Said otherwise, organize in order to succeed or if you want to succeed be organized.

An average but well organized team will beat any great players who are not well organized, any day of the week.

It is not as overwhelming as it looks. If you organize properly and monitor your statistics, **you can double whatever you are doing in less than five years; just by getting a 1% increase each month,** whether it be increased production, training, or what have you. But you can't do this if you are not organized.

If you want to succeed in any endeavor you must increase your organizational intelligence.

43. Ability to Strategize Intelligence

To strategize is a form of intelligence. The word strategize comes from the Greek word στρατος =army, which means to organize like a trained military unit to best win the battle.

For the most part, things in life are designed for the perceived average person without consideration of what is best for each one of us. Schooling is a good example. At age six children are expected to go to grammar school, at age twelve they all go to junior high and at eighteen they are supposed to enter college. Does this mean that all the children mature at the same age? Are they all ready to go to college at eighteen? Of course not. Some are, and others are not. So, do you follow this arbitrary route or try to figure out what is best for you and develop your own strategy? If you realized that you are not ready to go to college at age eighteen and you did a preparatory schooling for one or two years before you went to college, that would be called strategizing.

When an army of 10,000 soldiers is attacking your village of 500 able men, you must strategize to survive, even if this means to run away and fight another day. If you just accept fate and fight the battle because the mores of society claim that you must defend your village regardless, you and your people will perish.

If you believe in fate, you would not want to strategize. Instead you will just accept your fate. If you believe that you are a winner and always want to win, you would want to strategize constantly and to try to use all your resources and talents to best leverage them against the situation, endeavor or battle at hand. So strategize and win!

This concept is new to most people as they accept the systems that are set up for them and accept life as is. They accept their fate and instead of strategizing to survive and win, they end up with a much lesser gain.

This is similar to planning, but strategizing comes before planning. Strategizing is the master plan and planning are the details.

44. Planning Intelligence

Some people seem to be able to plan their lives from childhood to old age; others have no plan B if they get fired tomorrow.

Seeing different scenarios, different possible outcomes and figuring out the best one, is a highly cognitive skill not many possess. **The game of chess is a great example of planning as it requires this type of intelligence.**

To choose a particular grocery store to go shopping today, because it also has other stores around it that have things you need to buy as well, is another example of this type of intelligence. If you plan on having elective surgery when you will be off work, which is the same time a friend or relative is able to visit and help you out, you are again using this type of intelligence.

In college you learn that you don't have enough time to do all that is needed, so you learn to plan things out and do more with your time. You learn to do laundry, eat, and study all at the same time.

It has been said that in order to succeed you must have a plan and that without a plan, you planned to fail.

So always plan in order to succeed.

45. Ability to Prioritize Intelligence

This trait relates to the ability to discriminate and the goal intelligence. As you are pursuing your goals in life and try to make the best choices in terms of what path to follow and with what companions, a lot of stuff comes your way that demands your time and energy as they need to be handled. But you can't possibly handle the incredible amount of information and requests from other people coming to you constantly and therefore you must learn to prioritize, otherwise you will drown.

In our electronic society today we get constant bombardment of data. It is data, data, data. We can't possibly handle all these data nor should we, since a lot of it is useless anyway. We must handle only what needs to be handled and even for that we must prioritize, otherwise we will never reach our goals.

Have you ever wondered what it would be like to be a magazine or a newspaper editor who needs to fill hundreds of pages or so every single day, week, or month? Do they always have important data to tell people? Or do they just spin data to fill their pages? Of course, they do what they have to do to fill their pages. It is our responsibility to figure out if all this information has any importance, what to read and what to discard.

The same holds true for tasks that are requested from us every single day from many different sources. Everyone seems to vie for our time constantly. You need to know what is important for your goals and let the rest of it go. The simplicity intelligence dovetails here as well.

When you are in any kind of leadership position, people will not only attempt to take up your time directly but also indirectly by doing stuff that eventually will end up on your plate and need attention and require handling. My staff or even my kids will do some weird things. One of my kids got so mad at me a few months ago and called me a stupid idiot for something very minor. He is a good kid but his behavior made no sense any way you look at it. A great staff member just the other day said something to me that was totally inappropriate. Do I handle these weirdnesses or just let these comments go? In the above cases I decided to just let them go and made nothing of them. Why? Here are my thoughts.

People can be very peculiar and sometimes they seem to be run by demons. The majority of people worship four gods. These are the gods of greed, sex, fear, and ego, and at times they seem to worship all of them at the same time. You need to decipher constantly how to handle their everyday craziness. You need to decide what to handle and what to allow them to handle themselves. Yes, you can pick out and handle all their little nuances, but this will get you nowhere. In fact, it will surprisingly create more trouble to handle.

A book was written with the title "Don't Sweat the Small Stuff." This would apply here. You have to decide what is small and what is big, but for sure there are a lot of things coming your way and you need to always look at the big picture and prioritize constantly in order to survive and succeed.

So, the moral of this intelligence trait is constantly lay out the BIG PICTURE for yourself, your family, and your company and use that, as your guide. Anything that does not fit the big picture gets dropped, disconnected, or ignored and that is how you prioritize to reach your goals.

No goal attainment is possible without this type of intelligence, so learn to prioritize or drown.

Chapter J

The Exchange Intelligence

46. Willingness and Ability to Exchange Intelligence

Exchange is your ticket to life's game. If you don't have anything to exchange with people, they have no use for you. The greater you exchange with society the greater the benefits others will give you in return.

Poverty by and large is a result of poor exchange. Poor people are poor because what they offer to society is not unique or highly desirable or not offered in sufficient quantities and therefore society rewards them poorly. The unique part can be artificially and inappropriately enhanced by monopolies but more on that in another book.

What can you exchange with society? You find this out by direct observation, by reading books, and by asking the following question: What product or service can I provide to the world considering my talents and resources? Don't assume that you know. Survey and find out what society is actually willing to pay for what you are planning on giving. Your grandfather might have made a great living being a horseshoe repairman and he can teach you the trade, but I doubt you would be able to make a good living today as a horseshoe repairman. Regardless, you need to find out for sure.

This applies to all the types of exchanges in life, social as well as business. For instance, what was the exchange that brought you and your spouse together? What attributes or behavior did your spouse admire in you? Make sure you truly know and continue to possess these attributes in order to keep the same exchange in your marriage. You must really find out for sure, otherwise you are assuming things and your marriage will fall apart if you do not continue to exchange the things that brought you together in the first place. Although it is true that people change as they go through life, you might still be able to have the same exchange that brought the two of you together or if it changes make sure that both you agree to the switch. For example, if you had a mutual agreement for one spouse to be the homemaker while raising the children and the other spouse to work outside of the house, don't change this arrangement without another mutual agreement.

In another example (relating to employment exchange), you might like to make a philosophical, religious, or political statement with a big visible tattoo. That might be cool for you and your friends, but find out how much something like that can cut down your employment chances since most employers would not hire someone with a big tattoo, of say a swastika,[7] on their forehead.

Despite the feel-good speeches given by well-intended politicians or religious leaders, society rejects people who can't or are unwilling to exchange. Do not be fooled. This holds true always.

North American Indians were exterminated, in my opinion, because the Europeans felt that they had no use for them after the initial help the Indians provided. Rightly or wrongly, that is what they perceived.

The South American Indians on the other hand, for the most part, survived and flourished. Why? Because they exchanged with the Catholic Church. They became Catholic and the Catholic Church (the largest force in the land at that time) was happy with that exchange, spared them and supported them.

The Nazi scientists captured after World War II should have gone to jail, but they were brought to America and given great jobs, with great salaries because it was felt that they had important scientific knowledge the Americans could use.

---

[7] Swastika: 卐 the symbol used by the Nazis.

In a rather abstract example, what animals are becoming extinct? The ones who do not exchange greatly with humans. How about chickens, hogs, or cows? Are they becoming extinct? Of course not, they exchange greatly with humans and therefore continue to flourish and multiply in every land of the world.

The ability to keep exchanging with the world is the number one factor to your survival and success in life.

47. Willingness to Produce Energy and Products Intelligence

As mentioned in the previous trait, survival depends on exchange with other people. You need to produce products and services in order to exchange with others and in return you get money to buy products and services that you need. The wealth of a nation depends on the production of products and services by its citizens. The more you as an individual or as a country produce, the wealthier you will be.

Therefore, the intelligent thing to do in life is to constantly create energy within you despite outside circumstances and transform your energy into production of products and services for the benefit of all. Poverty? Hardships? Bad economy? Just reach deep down in yourself and produce energy to create products and services which are much needed by people and in sufficient quantity and somehow things will come out okay.

You would think that the above is just common sense. Yet today certain people promulgate the idea or the concept that wealth depends on governments printing money and allocating it toward certain directions. But all these concepts are lies. In order for wealth to be created we need to produce real products and services. Shuffling paper at some office, be it governmental or private, is not beneficial production, it is just busy work pretending to be producing something of substance. Frivolous lawsuits also are not producing products or services that help society.

Intelligent people do not wait for the government or the system to create fake wealth and fake exchange for them while they shuffle papers in some office; they constantly create energy and sweat to develop products and services for the benefit of society and consequently their own.

Οὐδεις ὤν ράθυμος εὐκλεής ανήρ αλλ' οι πὸνοι τίκτουσι τήν εὐδοξια.

No one who is lazy will ever have the chance to be famous or happy since fame and true happiness are the results of hard work.

--Ancient Greek Saying

48. Creative Intelligence

Here we have one's ability to create new products or services which society will find beneficial. **This can also be called the *Innovation Intelligence*.**

Look around you. Anything man-made was originally dreamed up by someone using this type of intelligence. Most people think that creating things is something other people do. Why? Any one of us has the ability to dream up and create new products, systems, processes, poems, songs, games, etc. These creations don't have to be complex. Some of the best innovations are so simple that when we see them in use, we say "Why didn't I think of that?"

Creativity starts with a dream, an illusion. An illusion is abstract, it's not even thin air. Do you validate it or do you ridicule it? It all depends on your self-confidence and the people you have around you. If you are surrounded by people who invalidate you or your creations, you will never demonstrate any creative intelligence. So, if you want to exhibit your creative intelligence, surround yourself with people who flow air into your sails and not people who stop the wind coming to them.

49. Money Intelligence

Money = it is what you get for exchanging goods and/or services with someone else.

Real money, as opposed to *MONOPOLY* money, is condensed energy and it represents condensed labor. For example: $100 in the United States in 2016 represents roughly all the energy/labor an average employee at McDonald's puts out for one day.

Real Money = stored labor = potential energy

There are people who are able to accumulate large sums of money and money seems to come to them the minute they are born. Their ability to think big and create all sorts of money making systems is what separates them from the rest of us. They are born with the idea that money belongs to them. Other people think of money as scarce and feel that they can't have much, no matter what they do.

The universe is built on energy and therefore it has enormous quantities of it. So why would anyone think that energy is so scarce when it is otherwise? One reason is because there are people among us who specialize in making it scarce for the rest of us. For an example on that, study the history of Communism. Communists turn rich countries into poor ones within a short period of time after they take over. They believe that money (energy) is scarce and that all they can do in regard to making things right (whatever that means in their minds) is to redistribute the existing money or energy found. They simply don't understand how money comes into existence and they make a mess of things.

Communists think that all the problems of the world are because of rich people. The real problem with rich people is that there are not enough of them.

Since money represents labor, the mishandling of money by governments is equated with the mishandling of labor, which triggers all sorts of things in people's minds. Things like suppression and slavery. Therefore, the mishandling of money has more severe ramifications than people realize.

As wealth is directly related to freedom, totalitarian regimes[8] must reduce the wealth of their citizens in order to succeed in controlling

---

[8] Totalitarian Political Regimes – where a small party controls all political power such as in communism, fascism, dictatorship, etc. The opposite is Democracy.

them. Poor people will accept a lot of suppression and control because their choices are limited. More on that in the Freedom Intelligences.

Energy is abundant in the universe and more can be made. This is proven by fission[9] and fusion.[10] Can you accept that energy is abundant and that you can have some? If so, then you can have money. If you think energy is scarce you will always have a poverty mentality.

---

[9] Fission - *physics*: a process in which the nucleus of a heavy atom is split apart

A large amount of energy is released when fission occurs. 1 + 1 becomes millions.

[10] Fusion - *physics*: a process in which the nuclei of atoms are joined. A large amount of energy is released when fusion occurs. 1 + 1 becomes billions.

Chapter K

Responsibility Intelligence

50. Responsibility Intelligence

It seems like everyone you talk to these days has a **lot of complaints** about everything and everyone. They complain about: the government, their job, their school, etc. **In general people feel the effect of their environment.** To remain the effect of your environment is not the intelligent thing to do. If you don't like your environment, then change it.

We are all responsible for the environment we find ourselves in and we all bear the responsibility to shape our world for the better. Our world is made up by the contributions of all the people in it. I write a book, you rebut it, another guy gets an idea from our discussion, which becomes instrumental in building a new system, etc. Especially with the advent of the internet, we can all contribute and affect things instantaneously, depending on our abilities, and what we can offer to the world. Pericles[11] said we must take responsibility for our political process. If we don't, then a few bad guys can pervert the entire process and turn democracy into slavery. More on that in the Freedom Intelligences.

---

[11] Pericles: Athenian Statesman (495 BC – 429 BC), considered the father of democracy.

Some say everything in this world is for naught. I say nothing in this world is for naught. Everything you do has ripple effects everywhere. Hillary Clinton wrote a book saying that it takes a village to raise a child. Yes, indeed, but only if people in the village take full responsibility for the raising of the village children.

Do you want a better world? A better city? A better neighborhood? Then do the intelligent thing: take action and do your part, even if it is a small act, if that's the best you can do. It is far better than what others are doing, which is nothing.

Don't complain about your spouse, handle him or her. Stop complaining about your children, correct them. Don't put up with bad politicians. Change them. Take full responsibility for everything around you and sooner than later you will find yourself in a better place. It's the intelligent thing to do.

Intelligent people take full responsibility for their environment and constantly shape it to their desires and therefore survive well in it.

51. Ability to Complete Actions Intelligence

I enjoy people who have this ability. You talk to them and they think in terms of completing the actions started and getting the results within the time and date these are needed by.

On the other hand, I dislike dealing with people who talk my ear off without an end in mind. When pushed to make a decision they blame others instead of taking action. They blame me, they blame the system and on and on. I say to them: "What do you propose?" They say: "Well, we should discuss it," as if we were doing something else. They just can't decide and therefore cannot complete the action they are in the middle of. As salespeople, if they sell the product they can't get the money and they just keep talking, or will not schedule the next step that is needed to deliver the service or product.

The point of responsibility comes in here as well, as this relates to the previous trait. If one decides and takes action, that means he also takes responsibility for those decisions and actions. If one does not want to take responsibility for anything, then he just keeps on talking and therefore never does any actions for which he can be held responsible.

The Greeks have a saying, “too much talk is poverty.” That is because society pays for completed actions, not words and promises.

“Λακωνιζειν εστι φιλοσοφέιν”
To be Laconic[12] means to be a philosopher.
--A Spartan phrase

---

[12] Laconic = To speak directly and to the point (very concisely) without unnecessary words.

52. Ability to Promote Yourself Intelligence

Do you PR[13] yourself or are you low key? PR stands for public relations, meaning advertising and/or marketing.

There is a Greek religious saying: "Do the good deed and bury it in the sea" meaning: If you do something good for someone keep it between you and God, as no one else needs to know about it. In other words, don't boast about a good deed. This type of thinking pervades many cultures, but if you are good at something or you did a good deed why not promote yourself for your benefit and to further promote this kind of behavior to others for the benefit of society?

I can see in certain situations when you did something for someone and you don't want him/her to know that you were the benefactor; but to have an entire philosophy, to not tell society of your good works and to not promote yourself is silly. It does not help you and it masks the guy who does nothing good. So, don't hurt yourself and mask the guy who does nothing. Promote yourself on anything you can

[13] PR – Public Relations making good works known.

legitimately say you are doing or making from which the world could benefit. Believe it or not the world wants to know.

Perception about you by others is reality to them, good or bad. So PR yourself and make their perceptions of you good. PR is a science and by far the most important one when it comes to commerce. People buy the brand names, the perceived quality, the perceived trust, etc. All that is driven by a PR machine. It is only partially true that your product or service will PR itself because people listen to the PR machine: the rumors and any information which you or others put out to the public about you, your product, or service.

The intelligent people PR themselves for anything good that they do and make themselves well thought of by others; they do not bury their good deeds in the sea.

53. Ability to Learn from Mistakes Intelligence

"Το δις εζαμαρτειν ουκ ανδρος σοφου"

"The same mistake done twice is not a trait of a wise man."

--Ancient Greek Saying

As we all go through life and get entangled with stuff we invariably make mistakes, either because of lack of knowledge or due to improper estimation. As we pull back from the experience, we must extract knowledge about the experience and next time we must not make the same mistake. If we cannot do that then we are not wise or intelligent. A pertinent quote by George Santayana:

"When experience is not retained, as among savages, infancy is perpetual. Those who cannot remember the past are condemned to repeat it."

One of the most inaccurate phrases in the English language is: "People learn from their mistakes" or said otherwise, people need to make mistakes to learn about life. If this were true, then the bums in the street, who made the most mistakes, would be the wisest people and therefore the most successful among us, but they are not. That's because, contrary to popular belief, people do not learn from their mistakes. In fact, most people assign reason or cause of their mistakes to other people and other things. Therefore, they cannot learn from the experience since they have a faulty perception about it and because in their opinion they did not make any mistakes but think that other people did it to them. **To be able to learn from mistakes is an intelligence trait not many possess.**

This particular intelligence trait is not as much about one's ability to learn from his own mistakes, but mostly about one's ability to learn from the mistakes of others around him or the mistakes he reads about from reliable sources and especially biographies. There is simply not enough time during one's lifetime to learn all there is to learn by trial and error. Therefore, you need to learn most data about life from observation of other people's actions. It's about seeing other people's mistakes, and **being able to perceive all the different possible outcomes of different actions without having to live through them**.

There are mistakes in life from which you cannot recover from easily. For example, being unmarried and getting pregnant as a teenager. In this case, the chances of succeeding in life can be diminished. You need to be able to **perceive** how hard it would be for you to bring a child into the world unprepared without having to go through the actual process of making this mistake. Another example is drugs. If you fry your brain with drugs, there is no way to fix your damaged brain. Can you perceive that without having to actually do drugs to make that discovery first hand?

Therefore, telling children that they need to make mistakes in order to learn is not a winning formula. The winning formula is to increase the child's observational and awareness abilities to be able to perceive the pain and turbulence these mistakes can cause so that he can avoid them.

Being able to perceive the pain mistakes cause in life is your child's ticket to success. This awareness must be taught to the child by study and direct observation. If your child does not perceive life well and keeps on riding on your coattails without figuring it out on his own, he will most likely fail sooner or later.

How would you know if your child perceives life correctly? He will be asking the right questions. It is okay to spoon-feed the child information about things in life and make him aware of what each mistake can cause, but at some point the child's awareness must come up on its own.

Early on in life it is very beneficial to try a lot of different things and make small mistakes or have recoverable failures. This way you can find out what you like and in what you are good at. Trying different things out will also raise your confront level and will also help you find your talents. Usually your talents lie in the areas you are good at and in what you get the most enjoyment from doing. Once you find your special talent or talents then plow through on them and you will never have to work a day in your life. You will just be having fun creating and you will never think of it as work.

To be wildly successful in life you need to find your talent or talents early on, and without making unrecoverable mistakes, put all your might and efforts on them.

Chapter L

Freedom and Intelligence

A. FREEDOM AND INTELLIGENCE

Freedom is directly related to intelligence. An intelligent person by definition would be a free person. If you are not free how intelligent can you possibly become? For anyone to gain the necessary intelligence and be able to create in life he must first and foremost be free.

The corollary is also true. **If one is intelligent, he will make sure he remains free, otherwise if one allows others to enslave him then he can't possibly be very intelligent, can he?**

B. WHAT DOES FREEDOM DEPEND ON?

Freedom Depends on the Following seven Pillars:

1. ***The understanding that competition in life is constant***
2. ***The realization that we need Democracy and Free Enterprise.***
3. ***Responsibility***
4. ***Knowledge***
5. ***Ability***
6. ***Team Support***
7. ***Production***

These hold true for an individual as well as for a nation.

Life is a game. For any game to have interest, there must be competition. As such, one must realize that competition in the game of life is constant. If you think otherwise, it's like hoping that the other team will go to sleep. If it does, then you hope that the next team will also go to sleep, then the other one, and so on and so forth. As you see, the logistics are against you, so if you want to be free, accept that competition is and will always be constant. So, don't put your guard down.

Further, you must realize that everyone you meet has different viewpoints and different realities. If you think that some guy in charge of a totalitarian regime will be an angel or a saint and that he will have the best at heart for you and your family, you are very much mistaken. The smooth-talking politician is not as smart, able, or as hard working as you might think. To be free, you need democracy in order to **have a say so in your governance and a free enterprise system to have career and job options. Otherwise, you will be subjected to the viewpoints and ideas of others who might not have the best at heart for you, or, simply not able to see your potential.**

In addition, **you need to take responsibility** for your right to be free; NO ONE else will do it for you. If you give up that responsibility others will gladly use your slave labor. Therefore, you need to obtain the necessary **knowledge** that is needed to survive optimally in the environment you find yourself in and **gain the necessary abilities** required to maintain your freedom. Without the ability to be free, you will not be able to maintain your freedom, but you will soon be enslaved.

No matter how personally able you might be, you need a **proper team**, because life is a game, and games are played by teams. The best team wins. Said otherwise **you need allies**. Allies are not necessarily friends. Friends are not necessarily allies; they might just be friends.

But, you can't just sit there and look pretty in your team's uniform. **You and your team need to produce products and services to exchange with the world**. Exchange is your ticket to life's game. Without it you can't get in the arena. Thus, you need to produce goods and services in abundance as needed so you don't depend on others for survival.

If you check the above in life and throughout history, you will see that they hold true. If it is so, then the opposite would be the road to slavery.

C. WHAT DOES SLAVERY DEPEND ON?

When people talk of slavery in America, they think of racial slavery and something of the past. That's inaccurate. All peoples and races throughout the world have been enslaved, to a lesser or greater degree. The Greeks and Romans called the Northern Europeans barbarians and treated them badly. In turn, Greeks were enslaved by the Romans and the Ottomans.

Enslavement is the overwhelm and the inability to do something about it. Enslavement takes many different forms, some are less obvious than others. All enslaved peoples throughout history were enslaved because they were unable to protect themselves from the slave masters. The purpose of this book is to lay out the anatomy of slavery and how to protect yourself from becoming overwhelmed by others.

The seven necessary elements for slavery are:

1. ***Thinking that all competition is extinct or that it will be extinct soon.***
2. ***The absence of democracy and free enterprise***
3. ***Lack of responsibility***
4. ***Lack of knowledge***
5. ***Disabled people***

6. ***No team or a bad team***

7. ***Lack of production***

As mentioned in the previous pages, the logistics that all competition will stop in the universe are impossible. So, anyone telling you that competition or any plotting against you or your group has ceased forever is trying to put you to sleep for someone else's benefit.

There are many good people in the world who do great things for our society, but to think that a leader of a totalitarian regime will be an angel or a saint and that he will lead you to the promised land is a terrible miscalculation. Absolute power corrupts, always. To be free you need options. You need democracy and free enterprise. The Ancient Greeks, the founders of democracy and the concept of individual freedom, even had many god options. Without options, you will end up an animal in a stable; read *Animal Farm*. There you see that even among animals there are different viewpoints which do not align with what is best for all the animals. If you want to be an animal in a stable or a slave (same difference) then do believe that a leader of a totalitarian regime or any regime for that matter will know what is best for you and your family and further believe that he or she will look out for you, regardless of circumstances.

So, if you **don't take the responsibility** to educate yourself about life and freedom in general, you will **lack the knowledge** needed to be free and you will be **unable** to function successfully and therefore **not be in a position to produce** any valuable products or services to survive, but will be dependent on others for your survival. Also, if you act as a lone wolf and **without a team backing you up, you will be easily overwhelmed**. Lack of team support makes you vulnerable to the slave masters whose objective is to divide and conquer so that they can overwhelm you. Bad schooling, bad diet, misinformation, splintering people from their teams, such as in divorce and therefore broken teams (families) create **weak and vulnerable people** who will be glad to serve masters in the hopes of obtaining survival.

The most important ingredient for slavery is weak, unable or disabled people[14]. Able[15] people will always fight enslavement; disabled ones will gladly put on the handcuffs and accept any type of enslavement just to get a meal for themselves or their families.

The words slavery and slave master have very bad connotations in our society. So, if you are a slavery production unit you can't advertise

[14] Weak or disabled people: The people who lack some or most of the seven pillars of freedom.

[15] Able People: The ones who possess the seven pillars of freedom.

as such, but you must go under different names. Can you think of people or institutions who are instrumental in doing 1—7 above? Well, whatever name they go under, realize that they are slave creation units. Does bad schooling come to mind, etc., etc.?

Do you now see how, based on the above, that all the intelligence characteristics relate to freedom, even if indirectly? In an overall sense, another definition of intelligence could be the ability to be free and remain free.

Following are the intelligence traits that are **directly** related to freedom.

BODY HEALTH AND FREEDOM

a. Healthy Body and Mind

Body health is a somatic intelligence as it is mentioned under that chapter. But it deserves to be mentioned here as well as it directly relates to freedom.

If one does not take care of his body by exercise, rest, and healthy food, then one cannot possibly be free as he will be held down by a diseased body, which will affect one's spirit and his willingness to fight for freedom.

b. Drugs and Freedom

1. Medical drugs. Although medical drugs are helpful in many occasions one must realize that medical drugs for the most part do not repair the body, but rather do one of the following three functions:

    i. Kill bugs

    ii. Slow down a body process, such as a fast heart rhythm

    iii. Speed up a body process, such as a slow heart rhythm

Supplementing a missing element, such as insulin, usually falls under these three categories. Almost all drugs have side effects.

So, take care of your body, because if the body gets damaged, for the most part, drugs will not repair it, they will just provide support.

2. Street or Illicit Drugs. If you look at history, these drugs have been used to control entire populations. The Nazis were provided with enormous quantities of these drugs throughout the war. I guess that is how they "did not feel" the pain of the Russian winter. Hitler the "father of Germany" was a meth head. Have you seen how he looked at the end of his life? He was only fifty-five years old then.

Have you heard about the opium addiction of the Chinese during the turn of the century? Talk about controlling whole populations!

Am I saying you are controlled in some form or another if you are taking street drugs? Read history and you decide. If you are busy doing drugs, you are at the very least distracted and not able to see and judge what the politicians and other people in power are doing and therefore unable to stand up for your freedom.

Also, the effect of drugs on your body is only secondary to the effect they have on your mind and spirit, but more about that in another book.

Chapter M

Freedom Intelligence

54. Orientation Intelligence

To get anywhere you want to go to, you need to be fully oriented, otherwise you will go astray and be lost and never reach your destination. Disoriented people are by definition lost. They will follow any direction and go anywhere they are directed to go to or do nothing at all. They will act like deer in headlights and will be easy to manipulate.

The word orientation comes from the Greek word oros=mountain. The concept is to use the mountains around you as **reference points to orient yourself** so that you know exactly where you are at all times.

By orientation here I do not mean just physical whereabouts, but I encompass all sorts of other references in life, "platitudes and latitudes," *the mountains* (the orientation points of life).

To find out if one is fully oriented in life you would ask questions such as the following:

1. What is a galaxy?
2. What galaxy are we in?
3. Can you describe our solar system?
4. What planet are we on?

5. How far is our planet from the sun?

6. How big is our planet compared to the other planets and the sun?

7. How is our planet different than the others in our solar system?

8. What percent of our planet is covered by water?

9. What is the livable land of the earth?

10. How many continents is earth divided into?

11. What is the population of earth?

12. What country do we live in?

13. What is the population of our country?

14. What is the land mass of our country compared to the world?

15. Which are the top ten countries in the world in relationship to population, wealth, resources, land mass, etc.?

16. Who are our top five trading partners?

17. Who are our top allies? How have they behaved in the past?

18. Who are our top enemies and why? How are we protected from them?
19. What is the population of our city?
20. What is the average wage in our country? In the world?
21. What is the average family income in our country? Our city?
22. What are the prevailing philosophies and religions on our planet?
23. What is the prevailing political system of our country and how does it compare to other countries?
24. What does our country stand for philosophically and politically?

I can go on and on, but you get the idea. I was shocked when I found out that highly educated people do not know the answers to most of the above questions. Some people excuse themselves by saying: "I don't need to know all these, it has nothing to do with my job" or similar excuses. But you do need to be fully oriented in life if you want to be free because disoriented people are easily manipulated. They are told falsities that are presented as truths and asked to support something that is detrimental to them but cannot discern it as such. Well, more about that in the next pages.

55. Political Intelligence

Political intelligence has to do with knowledge about governorship. If we as individuals and as a group don't have political intelligence, we will sooner than later become slaves despite all appearances.

Today almost everyone has the right to vote and we all feel good about it. But have you ever asked people if they understand the different political systems and how each system affects the economy and our individual freedom based on its proclaimed beliefs as well as historical data? In other words, do we know what will happen to us, in terms of freedom and our financial wellbeing, if we vote for say communism as opposed to voting for a party that supports free enterprise?

You will be shocked to know that most people can't define what each political system is, let alone how each will affect their lives. Most people in the Western World who support Communistic ideas think that if the Communist party came to power they will continue to have Democracy, free elections and the ownership of their businesses and home. If you don't believe me, ask your peers and you will get the same scary answers I got when I did my survey.

That is a reason I wrote the book *Political Systems and their Relationship to Economics and Freedom*. A great book if I may say so and a must read by all the people who want to live in a free and democratic society.

America today is proud of its democratic system. But do we as Americans know what is required from us in order to sustain a democracy? Democracy was invented in Greece and realized its height during the Pericles era, the Athenian statesman who is considered the Father of Democracy. He proclaimed in one of his famous speeches, the "Epitaph", written by the famous historian Thucydides, that **people who are not involved in the political process are not pacifists but useless.**

Therefore, according to Pericles, the Father of Democracy, if you don't possess political intelligence and you are not politically active, you are useless. Political = comes from the Greek word Polis = city, therefore political = civic. To be politically involved then, means to mind the civic affairs of your city, town or country.

To quote President Obama on his speech to the Greek parliament in 2016: "For it was here, twenty-five centuries ago, in the rocky hills of this city, that a new idea emerged. Demokratia. Kratos – the power, the right to rule – comes from demos – the people. The notion that we are citizens – not servants, but stewards of our society. The concept of citizenship – that we have both rights and responsibilities. The belief in equality before the law – not just for a few, but for the many; not just for the majority, but also the minority."

Americans shed much blood, sweat, and tears to defeat fascism during World War II and communism during the Cold War, but I doubt that the average American today can even define fascism, communism, or democracy and how each will affect their everyday life if it prevailed.

People today talk about Chinese capitalism. They don't know that it is actually a pseudo-capitalism under a communistic system in which not many freedom-loving Americans would like to live. I personally have not seen many Americans or Europeans rushing to immigrate to China. In fact, the opposite is taking place. A lot of the Chinese elite are leaving the "Chinese miracle" as soon as they can. See the *Economist*, July 2016.

If you ask people the question "What made America great?", most will give you strange answers that have nothing to do with free enterprise and democracy. I felt a sense of disappointment and fear when I conducted this research as I got some scary answers. If we don't know what caused our success, we can't keep on being successful . . . can we?

America became a great country due to its philosophical belief in the freedom of the human spirit and democracy. That translates into Freedom of Religion, Freedom to create in a Free Enterprise economy, and the ability for people to have a say in their governance.

What is the difference between successful and unsuccessful countries? It is their political systems. It is the one thing that affects how we live and behave more than anything else. I can fix any economy anywhere in the world if I can fix their political system to support true free enterprise. For more details, read my book *17 Rules or Laws to Fix Any Economy Anywhere in the World.*

There are people who assert: "You don't need to care or know much about all these issues or the overall political process in order to live well and make a lot of money. You can make money and do well in any environment no matter who is president and no matter the political system." Really? Many people in Greece, Venezuela, Argentina, and Cyprus were saying the same thing a few years back. Now they know better as they are fleeing their countries for greener pastures.

Look at history and you will see that the prevailing political and economic system of a country affects people more than anything else, regardless if some people assert otherwise.

If we don't take responsibility for the political system in our country and a bad system (such as communism) prevails, then we are not very intelligent, as we will be impeded from solving our problems in life and we certainly will not be able to capitalize on opportunities as there might be none!

In paraphrasing Pericles, I say: "Don't be useless; increase your political intelligence for the benefit of all."

56. Economic or Financial Intelligence

The word economy is derived from two Greek words oikos and nomos, which mean house and rules respectively. Therefore, economy means the rules or laws of the house or the country. In today's world, we associate this with just the rules about money, which I guess affect everything else.

Financial comes from the word fine, which is derived from the Latin word fin = finish as it pertains to completed or finished transactions. The word financial as is used today is: anything pertaining to money.

So, how is your intelligence about the "rules of the house" regarding money or finances? If it is high, then good; but if you are not highly intelligent about economics and finance, you can easily be manipulated about these subjects.

Let's see then how well you do regarding these subjects as we look at some "rules of the house" and let's start with your own house.

Most Americans own their home and they consider it one of their assets. Also, most have a mortgage on it through a bank. Did you know that the bank that holds your mortgage considers your house to be their asset too? How could this be? Further, have you noticed how you pay most of the interest up front? Like during the first ten years or so? How come?

On a different subject, the 10 o'clock news announces that the stock market went up today since the Dow Jones[16] jumped 2%. You hear that and think that the overall U.S. stock market went up 2%, right? But did you know that there are thousands of companies listed and traded in the U.S. stock exchange and that The Dow Jones is an index that tracks only 30 of these companies? So, the assertion that the stock market went up today because the Dow Jones was up is misleading, isn't it? Did you know that? If so good, but you are in the minority.

Regarding the Dow Jones or the S&P[17] 500 your broker says that over a period of so many years they each went up so much, etc. Well, did you know that they constantly change the companies the Dow Jones and the S&P track? The Dow Jones today only has in it just a few of the companies it had fifty years ago. New ones have been added as others were dropped since they ceased to be the largest companies or they went

---

[16] Dow Jones = An index that tracks the largest 30 U.S. companies.
[17] S&P= Standard & Poor's. Another index that tracks the top 500 U.S. companies.

out of business altogether. So, what really went up since most of the original companies are no longer there?

On a different subject, have you noticed how the prices of goods and services rise over time? This is called inflation. But do you know what causes inflation? How does it come about? How does it affect your investments?

On the subject of inflation do you know what Q.E. is? What is the difference between Q. E.$_1$, Q. E.$_2$, and Q. E.$_3$? Would you agree to a Q.E.$_4$? Most people have no clue of what Q.E. is, let alone how it affects us. Q.E. stands for Quantitative Easing. It is a fancy and convoluted term used for the creation of money (mostly credit) by the Federal Reserve and lending it to banks for them to make loans to the public to boost the economy after the economic crisis of 2008. What does this mean in plain English? It means the creation of money out of thin air (therefore fake money) which waters down your savings; the real money, that you earned by actual labor which you exerted to produce goods and services. That is what Q.E. really means, yet the majority of U.S. citizens have no clue. You ask: "Why don't they call it printing money out of thin air instead of calling it Q.E.?" Good question! Why don't they? That is why you need to increase your financial and political intelligence.

The printing of money out of thin air by the central banks (Federal Reserve in U.S.) without increased production is one of the main reasons of inflation.

As a <u>simplistic example</u>, if there is one trillion dollars circulating in the economy and the central bank prints another trillion dollars out of thin air, without any actual increase in production of goods or services, then you have twice as much money in the system chasing the same goods and services. Therefore, the prices of all things will double and you will get 100% inflation. Also, said otherwise, your savings will lose 50% of their buying power or that the government siphoned 50% of your savings (same difference), because of this money printing scheme mentioned above.

I know there are other factors involved and it does not work out this simplistically, but the above is a good example to think with.

In another example, how do you feel about the **minimum wage**? Do you feel that it should be raised? Or lowered? We have millions of people on each side of this argument. Each side is very convinced of the correctness of its viewpoint. One side says people need to make more money to live on, and who can argue with that? It only sounds fair. The opposing side says if we raise the minimum wage, people will lose jobs, but it does not explain why and how. So, which side is right and why? Well, let's analyze this further.

To offer to raise the minimum wage and *give* voters more money is a good campaign promise, but it is misleading at best because **you can't talk about minimum wage unless you add five other elements on the table.**

These five elements are:

1. Trade deficits
2. Government debt
3. The printing of money
4. Welfare
5. Monopolies

Let's analyze each and see how they relate to the minimum wage puzzle.

1. Trade Deficit

If as a country, we **allow trade deficits** with other countries, then by raising the minimum wage we will increase the loss of jobs in our country and therefore increase unemployment. We will look at this using China as an example, a country with which we do have a large trade deficit at this time.

As you observe the graphic depiction of this example below, let's suppose that each arrow represents $100 billion worth of trade.

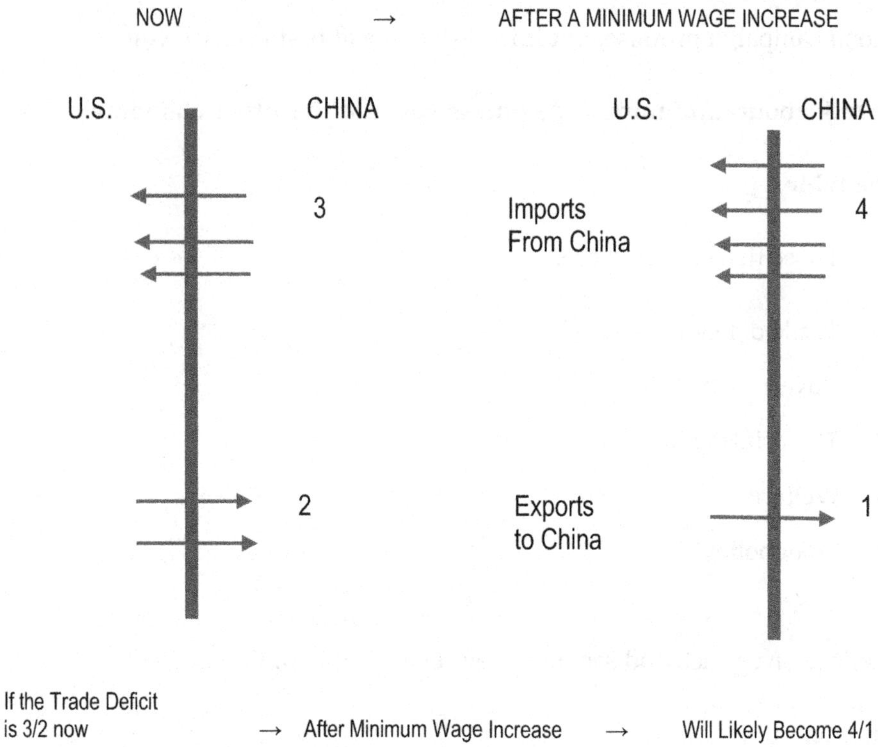

If we raise the minimum wage, then the labor costs in America will increase and consequently the goods and services produced in America will be more expensive. If we continue to have **free trade** with China, imports from China will increase even more and exports to China will decrease further, because while the cost of their products stayed the same, ours got more expensive due to the hike in our labor costs caused by the minimum wage increase. Although some Americans will earn more, due to the increase in minimum wage, others will simply lose their jobs since many American companies will invariably go out of business due to their inability to sell their now more expensive stuff to China or other countries.

The media and the politicians have conned people into thinking that free trade among countries is the ultimate nirvana. In my opinion, **free trade among countries is an oxymoron.**

Trade among countries in general is a wonderful thing and we should strive to increase it. Increased trade makes for a diverse, sharing and safer world, but **free trade with any country that creates trade deficits for long periods is very bad and ultimately debases your economy.** If you allow trade deficits, then why have an army; just allow the other country, the one you have long-term trade deficits with, to own you. They will, sooner or later.

Raising the minimum wage and continuing to have unregulated trade (free trade) is not workable unless the government is not allowed to go in debt or print money ever, in which case any trade deficit will self correct in a few years.

2. **Printing money.**

If the government can print money out of thin air as in Q.E., and increase the money supply in the economy without increased production it will ultimately cause inflation. Said otherwise, printing and dumping more money into the economy without increased production will increase the prices of the goods and services an economy provides because there will be more money chasing the same goods and services. So, if the government increases the minimum wage while at the same time is printing money to pay for it, the **whole thing is a farce because there is no real improvement in the buying power of the minimum wage earners,** despite their increased wages, since goods and services will now cost more.

3. **Government debt.**

The government has no real money, **it only has the power to tax people who have money** or who work and earn money. Borrowing then is an admission by the government that it cannot make an economy good enough to offer its citizens the things it has promised, such as an increase in minimum wage.

By the way, government debt is always borrowed against future generations' labor. The future generations, of course, are our children and grandchildren. When you advocate for the government to borrow money to offer its citizens more goods and services today, such as an increase in minimum wage, you are essentially advocating to borrow from your children and grandchildren in order to have a good life today at their expense, and to their detriment.

You want to increase the minimum wage? Fine, but don't go in debt to do so, otherwise you are stealing it from future generations.

4. **Welfare**.

I am not against welfare as a concept as I can see how people can end up in hard times, and we can all use help at some point in our lives; but **you can't have welfare and minimum wage at the same time.** Here is an example that explains why:

Let's say someone comes to my office seeking employment. I like him and I decide to hire him, but I realize he can't do much, either because he is mentally challenged or because he is very uneducated; so, I figure that I could start him with say $5 per hour, give him some chores and see how he does. I check with my accountant who tells me that by law I can't pay him $5 per hour and that he will cost me about $20 per hour. When I ask why, he says because the minimum wage law dictates that I pay this prospective employee $13 per hour, the minimum wage in some states, and then add FICA, unemployment and medical insurance, mandatory training etc., which will add up to over $20 per hour. Right away, in this hypothetical scenario, I realize that I can't take a chance on this guy if he ends up costing me $20 per hour. It will not be cost effective for my company; therefore, I decide against hiring him and I don't give this person a chance. Disappointed, he looks for a job elsewhere but can't find anyone to hire him due to the same considerations, so he goes and applies for welfare.

The same government that enforces the minimum wage approves him for welfare and forces my company and others to pay for it. The weekly welfare check that the government gives this unemployed person is roughly $5 per hour x 40 hours per week. In other words, the same I was willing to pay him for doing work for my company. You see, I had offered this guy $5 per hour to start, plus training, plus the possibility of advancement. The government says no, not allowed, but it forces me and other employers to pay this person $5 per hour without him doing anything to enhance my company, i.e., our staff who are paying his welfare check. Further, he is not learning any skill and certainly has no chance for advancement. How does this make any sense? It does not.

Do you now see then that having minimum wage and welfare at the same time is an oxymoron? It is only there to make people feel good with the illusion that the government is taking care of them.

5. Monopolies and Oligopolies vs. Free Enterprise

If you have monopolies as opposed to free enterprise and fair competition, then worker wages are set artificially by the monopolies and do not represent the true value of a worker as it happens in a true free market economy. Monopolies are created by big companies, the government and unions.

By the way, business monopolies and oligopolies promote free trade and cause trade deficits without regard for the well-being of their country. They want to develop products cheap elsewhere and bring them to America to sell them for a high profit. If Americans have no money, they facilitate for them to borrow it. This happens mostly via the government borrowing the money (from future generations) and giving it to the people through various channels mostly via banks through loans and credit cards to increase their purchasing ability through increased credit.

If we allow monopolies and oligopolies to cause trade deficits, then wages will be very suppressed with a bleak long term outlook and the free market will not work to raise everyone's standard of living as it should. Therefore, people will complain and the government, instead of handling the trade deficits or creating a freer enterprise system and a better economy, raises the minimum wage as a knee-jerk reaction, to keep people from complaining, which further creates more problems since it did not solve the real underlying problems of the economy.

You see, **I am not arguing for or against raising the minimum wage**. All I am saying here is that we can't talk about minimum wage, let alone take a position on arguing about the subject, if we are not at the same time addressing the five elements presented above.

I know this was a long explanation of one socioeconomic subject, but I wanted to make the point about needing to be economically and politically intelligent for us as voting citizens to make the right decisions. I chose this subject because it encompasses so many financial and political elements.

Some will say: "But these are very difficult subjects to put in front of the average person. Each person is doing his job; they are not economists". My answer is: "Yes, but they are voting citizens and they are presented these subjects by the politicians and are expected to vote on them directly or indirectly. So, the voters need to be educated to carry out their civic duty in a democratic political system." Unless of course one is advocating on manipulating the people and not taking their votes seriously and destroy **the most important thing people have, which is their ability to have a say so in their governance, which is the democratic system, the only guarantee of individual freedom.**

Pericles in "the Epitaph" brags about the citizens of Athens on how they are involved in the political process. He says: "we the Athenians tend our jobs but also make time to mind our political affairs."

Therefore, Pericles, the Father of Democracy, tells us that to have freedom and democracy we need to make sure all citizens are involved in the political process, at least anyone who votes. But to be involved you must be educated on the pertinent subjects, which essentially comes down to being informed about politics, economics, and life orientation.

Unfortunately, today, real education about these subjects is largely ignored by our educational system and the media. Therefore, people are made to believe that these subjects are not important or necessary to know. The motto of our current civilization is: "If something is not on the 10 o'clock news or if it is not taught at schools, it does not exist or it must not be important." Alas, there are many things that are important in this world that are not covered on the 10 o'clock news or taught at many schools.

Let's delve into this subject further then and discover why the public is not educated about these issues. This I believe has to do with the intention and the purpose of our educational system.

Although there are many different schools of thought regarding education, they can all be categorized into two educational systems or schools: (a) The **Greek or classical** one and (b) **the one born out of the industrial era.** Of course, you can also have school systems whose philosophy is somewhere between the two.

Now let's see how these two educational systems came about and how they affect us today. The word school comes from the Greek word σχόλη which means time off or break. The Greeks educated themselves on their off time so to speak out of curiosity and interest. Philosophy, another Greek word comes from the word Philos=friend and Sofia=wisdom. Therefore, a philosopher is one who is seeking wisdom.

People in ancient Greece went to school to obtain wisdom and not a job. They aspired to be wise about life, i.e., they were philosophers.

In order to be a philosopher, or wise (same concept) you must be well rounded in all the subjects of life including the sciences and encompass as many of the intelligence traits as possible. That was the concept and purpose of the Greek educational system. In fact, if you read about the ancients, Pythagoras, Plato, and the rest, they were all educated in many different. **These well-educated individuals, predominantly in Athens, created a political system in which its citizens had a say so in their governance. Thus, democracy and individual freedom came about. A system completely different from the rest of the world back then and most of the world today.**

This system **developed naturally** since you had **educated citizens** who as a consequence of their enlightenment wanted to have a say so in their governance, and demanded individual rights and the freedom to create without the interference of government or a church.

This Greek educational system, which was based on the idea for people to be philosophers, carried over to northwest Europe and eventually to America under the banner of **classical education** that all elite students of the aristocratic families would espouse. They intended to be well educated in all aspects and disciplines of life. They aspired to be philosophers themselves. Therefore, they studied the classics, Greek and

Latin, also history, politics, philosophy as well as a profession, such as medicine or law.

This system created a critical mass of people, same as in ancient Athens, the American forefathers, who, philosophers themselves, naturally sought self-governance and individual freedom, i.e., democracy. **What did the ancient Athenians and the American forefathers have in common? A critical mass of well-educated citizens naturally seeking individual freedom, and a say so in their governance, thus democracy was born in each place.**

On the other hand, during the same era, the children of the common people, the commoners, who were the great majority, were not sent to school, but worked in the fields. This went on for eons until the rise of the industrial era where we had the advent of machines, factories, and a great deal of infrastructure. Who was to build and maintain all these dirty and dangerous machines and infrastructure? The aristocrats were therefore forced to school and train the commoners' children to run and maintain the machines, help build the factories and the necessary infrastructure. But, they didn't have to give them a well-rounded education; all they had to do was build mass production schools to teach them, to build and run the machines and the infrastructure. Thus, **The Educational System of the Industrial Era** was born.

Under this system, which was carried over to America, you send people to school not to be philosophers or to be educated in the full sense, but for them to be trained in a specific subject and graduate them with a degree of being *mechanics* in that subject and nothing more. The student would spend enormous amount of time learning about machines or how to fix roads or build buildings or a branch of medicine, but learn very little about real economics, politics, geography, world affairs or the like. Why should he? It was not his business. Those subjects were the domain of the aristocrats not the commoners. The non-aristocrat was considered another machine and therefore easy to manipulate.

Well, that is fine and dandy if you intend to have an aristocratic system or an oligarchy, but **this school system does not create educated citizens needed for a true democratic society.** No wonder people today are so disillusioned about the workings of democracy. It's because we don't have educated citizens. The average college graduate today does not know the answers to half of the questions posted on the Orientation Intelligence list, let alone true data about politics and economics.

When the public in general is not educated about the subjects of politics, economics, and life orientation, it opens the door to misleading the people on these most *important to life* subjects.

Misleading people is part of enslavement and the opposite of intelligence.

How do you mislead people? Easy. You give them false data or no data on the freedom intelligence traits and then you can direct them any way you want to. This is mostly done via the media. **The fact is that any lack of knowledge about politics and economics and other important to life subjects will be used against you.**

If I was to pick the top subjects people are misled or uninformed about in our society I would choose the following four:

1. **Little or no education on life orientation** (Trait #53 – Orientation Intelligence).
2. **Little or misleading education on politics. (**Trait #54 – Political Intelligence).
3. **Little or misleading education on economics, money or how politics and economics are interrelated** (Trait #55 - Economic or Financial Intelligence).

4. **Purposely ignoring actual statistics of organizations and people**. For example, the media wants to promote Joe Smoothtalker and portrays him as a nice guy and claims that he is trying very hard for the country; but, purposely ignoring his actual statistics prior to getting this job and never looking at the statistics since Joe Smoothtalker came on board. Did the statistics of the organization or the post he took over go up or down? Why on earth are we ignoring that? The orchestrators ignore the actual statistics of the people they promote, purposely, because they don't want you to base your decision on actual statistics; they want you to follow their lead on whom to support. **They want you to vote for the guy <u>who they claim that will be able to do the job</u>** and not for the guy who has done it. You see, the guy who <u>can do</u> and <u>has done</u> is too proud to be bought and be pushed around by special interests. The guy who just talks a good game without the ability to do, will accept anything assigned by the orchestrators.

As this is a book on the traits of intelligence and how to raise one's intelligence and therefore his ability to be free, **we promote the**

classical educational system and not the narrow-focused training method born out of the industrial era.

If after reading about these subjects you feel overwhelmed, do not despair. The basics of these subjects are very easy to obtain. I can teach anyone the basics of politics, economics, and life orientation in just a few months. So why are these subjects presented to the public with so much complexity? Good question; read my book *Political Systems and Their Relationship to Economics and Freedom* and find out more about that.

To be intelligent you must remain free. Therefore, you need to be a philosopher and to constantly be seeking knowledge about life and take responsibility for things all around you and not just be a mechanic in some field.

For those who can't quite see how these political and economic topics have to do with intelligence, let's look at one genius of intelligence, Nikola Tesla. During his lifetime, Tesla was awarded about seven thousand patents; that is an astronomical number of patents in the difficult field of electrical engineering. By itself this makes him a god of electrical engineering and more. But how smart is it if you or I can do that and all our patents are taken and used by sinister people and we die paupers in obscurity? For my part, this is not very intelligent regardless of any number of patents you or I amass. See our original definition of intelligence.

Chapter N

Abstract Intelligence

The following traits I put under the category of abstract[18] intelligence traits. They are abstract in the sense that they encompass and describe abilities not as easily understood by all and are certainly not well described or defined.

These abilities, although abstract, are nevertheless intelligence traits, which the geniuses of our world seem to be endowed with; some more than others. Let's explore them and learn more about them.

---

[18] Abstract = Not easy to understand because of being extremely complex, remore from concrete reality

(Webster's New World College Dictionary, 4th Edition)

57. Imagination and Visualization Intelligence

Our everyday world is made up by the contributions of all the people in it. This we call the real world. And although we all have had some part in it, the world is so vast and our contributions seem so tiny that it makes us think that we don't matter and that we exert no control over it.

But, via imagination and visualization we can create an entire world in our own mind, which is 100% our own creation and therefore fully controlled by us. In fact, anything created in the real world, was originally started in our imagination first. That is actually how it works. In order for us to start anything — a relationship, a business a new system of things — we put it together in our own mind first. There, we grow it, alter it, test it, and then we try to project it into the physical world or real world if you will and try to make it a part of it. Without this "internal laboratory" for one to put forth his own ideas and creations, nothing would be possible in the physical world. Tesla, the great electrical inventor, could visualize entire engines and see them running in his mind and then could put their design on paper to bring them forth in the real world.

Without imagination and visualization our own world would be a very depressing place, especially for children. Imagine children forced to deal with adult reality all the time. They would be depressed, and would not be able to be playful children.

Imagination and visualization are abilities needed for our survival, present and future, and without them we would be like robots lacking any creativity. So go ahead; imagine and visualize all you want and create a better product, a better place, a better future. It is your own space, your own world. Do as you please, create away and extrapolate it in the physical or real world for the benefit of all.

58. Incubation Intelligence

Incubate:

a. To cause embryonic development

b. Develop and hatch

(*The American Heritage Dictionary New College Edition*)

Incubation Intelligence is the ability for one's mind to cook up solutions for a problem posed to it. **Have you noticed how after you pose a problem to your mind, it seems to go to work on it, incubating (cooking up) ideas over the next several hours, days, or months, and furnishes you solutions, which can be helpful toward solving this problem?**

That is incubation intelligence. It is the ability of your mind to come up with solutions about problems you are trying to solve.

It is different than the Visualization Intelligence in that this is involuntary. Visualization Intelligence is something you actually have total control over and you can actively visualize whatever you wish. Incubation is something your mind does all on its own it seems, same as the hatching of eggs, and any possible direction from you appears to be subconscious.

Experience, having read a lot, having lived a full life, being able to think for yourself . . . all of these are helpful toward this type of intelligence and the more you possess these traits, the greater your incubation ability becomes.

Some people have this ability in spades to the point where they feel that they are in touch with the cosmos or that they are getting messages from the gods. Others don't even know what I am talking about.

I believe we all possess this ability, but most of us are not trained to tap into it.

59. Ability to Unplug and Be in Your Own Space Intelligence

Life is a constant movement of huge streams of energy and time, running at various speeds. Some people call these the stresses and pressures of life. All of us, and especially the most able among us, run at high speeds in all directions, mentally and physically. Things can get very intense as one is burning the candle at both ends, but one cannot keep this up forever. The ability or intelligence to unplug from this stream of energy of time and stress is a high level ability and it can help one mentally and physically.

When I was a child I could not take naps. I would see my siblings sleep for one hour in the afternoon, unplug so to speak, and be very refreshed after that. I, on the other hand, was very stressed and tired. This went on until my third year of dental school. Then perhaps I felt that I had found a profession I liked or that I got a better understanding of the world, which possibly caused me to be more relaxed about things; but it was not until age twenty-five when I could take naps at will and be refreshed.

Thomas Edison, I have read, used to be able to take naps at any time he wanted and come out refreshed.

Being able to take a nap or relax as needed is only one form of decompression or unplugging. There are many others. It's been written that Archimedes, Leonardo DaVinci, Albert Einstein, and Nikola Tesla were able to tune the world out and be in their own space and time or in another universe altogether.

Why is it so important to be able to step out of the time stream and into your own space? Well, take a look what the ancient Greeks had to say about that. The Eleatic School of Philosophy, Fourth century B.C. (ancient Greece) held as its tenet that the true being is singular and unchanging and that plurality, change and motion are illusory (*Webster's New World 4th College Edition*). So, according to them, change and motion, which relate to time and space, are illusions and are not real. Only you (the true being) is the only real and unchanging in the equation of life.

Therefore, to be able to step out of the illusions of time and energy into your own space, would be the ultimate truth which is you without time and motion. That state should feel right, relaxing, and stable.

As people read this, some will have no idea what I am talking about; others do have the ability to tune the world out as needed, and few have the ability to be in their own universe or another cosmos entirely.

The ability to be in your own time and space is a high intelligence trait, although abstract to some.

60. Ambition Intelligence

Ambition is the desire to reach a certain goal or to obtain a certain status, wealth, etc. **It's what drives one to do great things.** Why did I put this trait in the abstract category? Because it is a quality not easily understood or well defined, as most people think. Ambition has many shades and grades; one has the ambition to start his own business the other to conquer the world.

If I had one wish for my children that would be for them to have great ambition. **If one has great ambition he will force himself to improve on all the other intelligence traits.** He will find solutions to his problems and push through any obstacles.

Ambition is the driving force of life. Anyone who wants greatness must have great ambition first.

Great ambition transcends humanity and reaches spirituality and the gods. All great projects in life (Apple, Google, Microsoft, Alexander the Great's empire, the Great Wall of China) did not happen by chance. They were not accidents of circumstances as some collectivists would like you to think. They were forged by men with the greatest of ambitions and yes, greed! **These founders were trying to reach God Himself and believed that they would find Him in the process (more on that in another book). Did they reach God? Who cares. The fact that they believed they could and reached so high, benefited us all.**

Do we as a country desire greatness? Then we must encourage the ambitions of our citizens to make them into reality and allow them to reach as high as they can. Mediocrity gets us nowhere good. Mediocrity's goal is the rationing of what we already have instead of creating more.

So I say: let's reach for the sky, there is benefit to be had from that for all of society. Amen!

61. The Ability to Accept Simplicity Intelligence

I never thought I would be putting this down as an intelligence characteristic, yet it is an important one and necessary for success. What I discovered was that the majority of people are not willing to accept the simple truths in life, but look for the complexity in things and therefore get tangled up and as a consequence get sidetracked from their goals.

One of the reasons for this is that people want to feel important and they think a certain amount of complexity makes them and what they are involved with important. Otherwise said they think something simple can't be important. Due to this computation, many people want to do things in a complex manner or accept only complex answers. They therefore create complexity and reject simplicity. To make it more clear let's cite some examples. I went to school for over twenty years including professional school. So, I have an extreme amount of knowledge about schooling and how to do well at school. Naturally, I try to pass this information on to my children, that's simplicity. My children for the most part reject that simplicity and think I am too old to know and choose a more complex route to get their knowledge about school, instead of the simple advice coming to them at home from a parent.

In another example, some people do not trust their observation about things (a direct and simple way to obtain knowledge), and accept an untruthful complexity about the subject from an *authority* in a book or television. For instance, they can directly observe how the economy in their town or city is doing, but instead they choose to accept what the authorities are telling them about it on television or in the newspapers.

On a different scenario let's say you live on a ranch in the western United States and hear galloping animals outside. The simple thought should be: "animals are running outside, likely horses or maybe cows." The complexity would be to think: "animals are running outside, they could be zebras, antelopes, lions, horses, elephants, and perhaps alien species." Complex people think the second option and try to defend their position. These are the people whom when you ask a simple question such as: "Do we have any more coffee?" instead of answering with a yes or no (simplicity), they go on to convoluted explanations of how so and so did not get the coffee you requested or that the coffee machine is acting up, etc., etc., (a lot of complexity).

Simplicity has efficiency, beauty and intelligence in it. Complexity is inefficiency, stress and **no solutions.** Complex things are solved by breaking them down to simplicities. In fact, the main concepts of everything in life are pure simplicities. Can you accept that or do you want to be complex?

Another reason for complexities is to cover something up. In fact, a lot of the complexities we see in life are made up to cover lies or ignorance about a subject. How do you hide a lie? You cover up the simplicity of it, which is your bad deed, or your bad intention, or perhaps just your lack of knowledge about the subject, with a lot of complexity to the point where the other guy cannot see the simplicity in it (the real reasons) and is focusing on the complexity (the cover up), and therefore he does not suspect you.

A third reason for complexities and convoluted ways is due to an unwillingness to decide on a given situation. The motto becomes "let's talk about it instead of deciding to do something. And the more complex we make it the less likely it will be that we will have to do something about it."

The most intelligent of people look for the simplicities in life and not for the complexities in things, because simplicity is where the truth resides.

Thomas Jefferson, a very intelligent fellow, used to say: “Take life by the easy handle.” In other words, start with the simplicities.

Simplicity wins the day. Complexity might look important, but it will tangle one to oblivion.

62. Way of Thinking Intelligence

How do you think about things? Are you proactive or reactive? Do you get emotional first and think later? Or, do you think logically while controlling your emotions? Do you feel confident in your ability to solve the problems presented to you in life or have you decided that life's problems will overwhelm you?

Your thinking process about things and the problems you face in life determines the outcome, doesn't it? An intelligent thinker would handle life's problems using the following or similar thinking process:

He thinks: "I am intelligent and I can solve problems. In fact, I feel I can solve any problem in life and I can have fun doing so." Now let's see what we have here:

He observes the problem→He accepts what he is observing and analyzes the data which he then breaks down to simplicities → Thereafter he computes the observed data using logic without illogical emotion→He decides → then acts to solve the problem by starting with the easiest and most understood route → He then observes the results of his actions→Gets the feedback→Based on the feedback repeats same action or actions or alters his actions as determined by the feedback and the cycle is repeated. Sooner rather than later, he solves the problem or problems involved, learns from the experience and moves on to the next problem with more abilities and added confidence.

63. The Ability to Handle Good Fortune Intelligence

Most people hope for good fortune to come their way. They want to marry a prince or a princess, win the lottery, get drafted by a big sports team, or get a call from Hollywood. But have you noticed what happens to them when they get a great fortune, or a great deal of luck come their way? They don't do very well. In fact, most end up losing it! Not only do they lose their new-found fortune, but they end up in a worse position than before. Why is that? It is because they are missing the intelligence trait of being able to accept and handle a good fortune. Yes, this is indeed an ability and an intelligence trait, which some people have it, most do not.

Some people can't even handle an unexpected good day, let alone a great fortune. As such when something good arrives at their doorstep, whatever it is, they get rid of it and go back to their misery; as they cannot emotionally handle any greatness coming their way. They will "dispose" of it in a hurry, as they feel uncomfortable being happy, lucky or "tall and handsome". They feel undeserving of such luck, even if they are one hundred percent responsible for this fortune. Such people become easy prey for others who want to take advantage of their "lucky" position and try to get them to dispose of their "spoils", i.e., luck or fortune. They make them feel guilty and use that, to siphon their "luck" away for their benefit.

Along those lines have you also noticed how when you help certain people, they can't have it and don't seem to appreciate your help? That's because they feel overwhelmingly obligated to you and feel that they can't rise to the level of being able to exchange back with you. Why can't someone take the help and exchange back with his helpers? It's because he lacks the ability to handle a good fortune.

I hear some of my friends say: "So and so was lucky, he inherited millions from his family and that's how he got to be big today", meaning he/she does not deserve much credit for his lofty position because he was handed a great fortune and was not self-made. What they don't realize is that most people who inherit a great fortune cannot handle it and they either shrink it or lose it altogether. So, if one grew a fortune he inherited, he deserves a lot of credit as he possesses good fortune intelligence, besides other traits of course.

In terms of an intelligence trait, this one is more of an emotional ability and less about business acumen

64. The Unknown Factor Intelligence

What sort of intelligence trait is this you ask? Well, if I knew, it would not be unknown, would it?

When St. Paul preached the gospel in Athens, the Greeks told him that they already had an altar for his god. It was named "The altar of the unknown god." The Greeks figured that besides the gods they knew, there might be another god or gods they didn't know. So they reckoned, they might as well cover themselves (hedge their bets so to speak) and have an altar for any god they might have missed. You see even the ancient Greeks, who had laid out their divinities very carefully, knew that there are unknown factors when it comes to surviving in life, even unknown gods altogether.

A few years ago, I watched an interview, on television, of a coach who worked solely with Olympic athletes. What he said was something I always knew. He said that the Olympic athletes are not your everyday humans, but they possess special talents in order for them to be able to do what they do. He meant that they were born with a special ability and/or with a certain mindset to use their body so adroitly that they were almost superhuman in some somatic ability or abilities.

Michael Jordan is definitely athletic looking but I know a lot of people who look somewhat like him in height, weight, and muscle tone, but none of them can use their body like he did . . . not by a long shot. Why? We don't really know, do we? This is the unknown factor of intelligence.

Over dinner, billionaire investor Mr. John Calamos Sr., the founder of Calamos Investments, was trying to explain to me how when you focus on something with tremendous interest you can do miracles. He gave me as an example the time he joined the air force after college and how he learned how to fly, in a short period of time. He said to me: "I went from knowing nothing about planes to flying jet fighters in formation at night in just one year."

What Mr. Calamos does not realize though, is that there are very few people on the planet who can do what he did. I am sure his intense interest and focus helped him greatly, but there are other unknown factors (unknown to the rest of us and possibly himself) that propelled Mr. Calamos to have this ability, to be able to learn to fly fighter jet planes adroitly within just one year of study and training.

What propels these people to do what they do? We don't really know for sure. It could be genetics, it might be the right time and place for the exact talent to come forth, divine intervention, a guardian angel, or perhaps it was the help of a friend or family member who devoted his entire life to give another a special life; such as spending hours upon hours training this future star. It could be all of these and more. I don't know for sure, but I do know this: The *Greats* of our times and in the past were not your average Joes who tried hard. They either had special help or found themselves at the right time and the right place for who they were, whereby their rough diamond self became animated and developed into a glowing star.

I also know that the harder you try in life, the luckier you get, and that growth is not arithmetic, but geometrical, meaning that, as you push forward, progress accelerates. So the earlier you start the more time you have to accelerate.

Parents try to give their children an education and some sort of inheritance. Although these are good things to give to your children, the best inheritance you can possibly give them is the **ambition** to have a burning desire to rise to levels not reached before, for the benefit of all. Perhaps this is the unknown intelligence trait ... the ambition not only to overcome the wind against one, but to use it to soar to the sky and meet with the gods. Okay, I am getting a bit carried away here but I did say that these traits are abstract.

Chapter O

Application Intelligence

65. Application Intelligence

All the parts of intelligence are, for the most part, potential abilities and by themselves will most likely not create great success. **The ability to put these potential abilities to work I call the *Application Intelligence.*** It is the ability to put knowledge and resources, yours and other people's, to work on getting results and reaching one's goals.

Many people have abilities and know things, but most can't do much with them. Can you apply what you know? Can you put all the parts of something, be it a project or an idea, to work? This is the thing that separates the men from the boys. This is where the rubber meets the road so to speak.

Assuming you have leadership skills, you need the application intelligence to be a great leader. Also, the higher your leadership capabilities the greater the potential for the application intelligence to be used in a grander scale.

In fact, this intelligence trait requires great leadership skills in order for it to reach its true potential and without the leadership capabilities it will never reach any great heights. For example, if a scientist in the lab can take several inventions and put them together to create new forms, he exhibits great application intelligence. On the other hand, if he possesses little leadership ability he will be unable to lead a team of scientists to bring forth his invention on any grand scale.

For one to have both the leadership and the application intelligence traits highly developed, it means he is truly a giant among humans.

Application intelligence is what the world's leaders, especially in industry, possess in abundance. They take existing resources and technologies and put them together to create whole industries. They are the conductors of the orchestras of the world.

EPILOGUE

WHICH INTELLIGENCE TRAIT IS THE MOST IMPORTANT TO POSSESS?

Ideally one should possess all of them. But this seems to never be the case. Even the ancient gods did not possess all these traits, not by a long shot.

What if you had limited choices? Then it would depend on the time and place you are born in. In the distant past *Somatic Intelligence* was key; the tall, strong man would become king. Today, *Duplication* or *Book Intelligence* seems to pay the most. Our society places a great value on one's ability to duplicate and regurgitate information (at least in school and the academic circles, which play the biggest role toward success for the average person).

As for me, given limited choices, I would almost always go for the Leadership and the Application Intelligences. **The ability to apply what one knows and put everything to work, including other people's resources and be able to lead all concerned toward a result or a common goal, are ultimately the key factors to great success.**

How do we define success? My definition of success is as follows: **One is successful if one truly feels successful about his or her status**

or accomplishments in life. In other words, if you honestly feel you have succeeded in reaching your goals in life, **then by <u>your own standards</u> you are successful.** If, on the other hand, you are complaining about things and people and making excuses, then by your own admission, you are not successful.

Based on our original definition of intelligence, which is **the ability to solve one's problems and capitalize on opportunities in life**, an intelligent person would by definition be a successful person.

IS INTELLIGENCE DEVELOPED OR IS ONE BORN WITH IT?

A key question about intelligence is: Is one born with it or is it something that one develops as he grows up, goes to school, and learns from his environment?

I can best explain my viewpoint on this by using the following analogy with cars.

A Rolls Royce or a Mercedes are born from the factory as such, especially their engines, and they are not made by the environment afterwards. You can feed another car Rolls Royce or Mercedes type of fuel all you want, but the car will not become a Rolls Royce or a Mercedes. It will still be the same type of car, at least its "engine," it came into this world as. The environment (home, school, job, training, culture, etc.) will have an effect on the condition of the "car" and how it runs, but it will not change its type. A Rolls Royce is born a Rolls Royce; a Volkswagen is born a Volkswagen. Both are useful cars as different engines have different usefulness. I would use a Rolls Royce to drive in style, but I need a tractor to move a tree.

One's environment, i.e., his culture, family, and school, can affect how the *engine* is running and how well it is maintained. If the environment is bad, then any car, even a Rolls Royce, will be clogged up and it will be rendered useless. A Volkswagen in a great environment, where it is well taken care of, will have a well-running engine and it will be a great and useful car.

All the intelligence traits mentioned here can be improved upon just by reading this book. You should have increased your intelligence greatly if you studied this book with honesty and you got this far.

COMMON SENSE

When I showed this book to one of my friends he said: "I love it. It involves a lot of common sense." I explained to him that the problem with that phrase is the word **common**. Common means something that is well-known among people and therefore it's what is expected. But who made sure that:

a. The majority of people are taught a **certain knowledge** that we want to now call common? and

b. The majority of people agree with a certain **behavior** which we can, from here on out call common and expected behavior?

If a and b have not taken place, then there is no such thing as common sense or commonly expected behavior, as knowledge and behavior are not picked up by osmosis.

We have to teach everything to people and then make sure that they are in agreement with the data and that they make them their own before we can call them common.

YOUR CATHOLIC OR ALL-ENCOMPASSING INTELLIGENCE QUOTIENT SCORE

The word Catholic comes from the Greek word Καθωλικος which means:

All-encompassing or wholly. The Intelligence traits covered in this book are all encompassing the subject of Intelligence.

So, what is your Catholic or all-encompassing intelligence quotient? Here is how to figure out your score: You give yourself a grade from 1 to 10 for each intelligence trait presented and then you add up all the numbers for a maximum grade of 65 x 10 = 650, a grade only possible by God Himself.

Try it out and give yourself a grade for each trait and see what your all-encompassing I.Q. really is. My hope is that this book raised it for you by a large factor. The whole purpose of this book is to raise everyone's all-encompassing I.Q. for the benefit of all.

Reread the book at a future date, as it will seem like you read a new book then and you will raise your overall I.Q. even more.

Good luck and thank you!

Made in the USA
Monee, IL
15 October 2023

44480679R00136